Puffy Muffin

presents

Memories in the Making

Additional copies can be obtained at
www.puffymuffin.com
Puffy Muffin, Inc.
229 Franklin Rd., Brentwood, TN 37027
(615) 373-2741

ISBN 0-9753183-0-6
©2004 by Lynda Stone

Produced by Thomas Marketing Solutions
Design by Fussell Graphics • Printing by Classic Printing

Lynda and Jack Stone

DEDICATION

TO JACK

*My constant support, comfort and encouragement
for the 36 years we have been married.*

*I am certain I would not be the person I am today without your
wisdom and Godly direction for our lives together. Thank you.
I can confidently say that I am yours and you are mine.*

An interior view of The Puffy Muffin Restaurant and Bakery
Viewing toward the kitchen

Lynda began The Puffy Muffin in 1986 in Brentwood, Tennessee. By the late nineties, customer demands and operational needs far exceeded the initial space. After searching for several years for a new location, The Puffy Muffin relocated to an adjacent space that afforded almost triple the display, seating and operational capacity. The following friends are responsible for assisting Lynda in the layout, design and construction of the current space:

ARCHITECTURE AND SPACE DESIGN
Edwards+Hotchkiss Architects PC
Brentwood, Tennessee

CONSTRUCTION
Carden Company, Inc.
Brentwood, Tennessee

INTERIOR DESIGN
Kaye D. Frensley Interiors
Nashville, Tennessee

Introduction

The Lord loves us all very much. One of the ways He shows his love is to give us gifts. We all know what it is to receive a gift – it means it's free, no strings attached, it's a gift! "Hospitality" is one of the gifts He has given me. It seems to come easy for me to host guests, prepare meals and to make others feel welcome in our home. I can't take any credit for this – it's a gift! I suppose that's one of the definitions of a gift – something you don't have to work at because it was given to you. I want to share this gift with you.

Hospitality encompasses many things, but primarily it's the ability to provide a place of comfort and pleasure for your guests.

When I think about pleasure, my mind naturally goes to food! I wonder what that's about! Even in biblical times when a guest or even a wanderer was seen approaching, preparation was made for their comfort. Great preparation was made for the meal that would be their welcome. I like to remember the scripture that says we "entertain angels unaware." What an honor!

But how can you manage a house full of company if hospitality isn't your gift? Don't stress – help is here! One way to begin is to start with 'tried and true' recipes. Look to your grandmother and other relatives. Ask them to share their entertaining experiences. It will be a blessing and you will come away with real treasures.

I presume there are original recipes out there, but more than likely what is passed on to you will be a new twist on an old thing. This should encourage you to put your special touches to old recipes...I think this is a mark of a good cook. Make it yours in your own special way.

Hospitality can also be shown by being sensitive as to whether or not your guests are enjoying themselves. Sometimes the most basic meal will bring the most joy. It isn't necessary to prepare 'fancy' foods to be considered a good cook.

You are making memories in your home, so go for the sights, sounds, smells and tastes of the familiar. This is what memories are made of. Listen to your family and the things they remember about a holiday, or a particular recipe they want you to make for the family reunion. "Mom, you make the dressing for Thanksgiving," or "Let Aunt Lulu bring the relish tray." Speaking of the relish tray, for some reason this is a big deal at our family gatherings! You just open jars and cut up vegetables and – voila! You have a relish tray. But ironically, tradition perhaps, the relish tray takes front and center with our family. There must be the small sweet Gherkins, black olives, little grape tomatoes, baby corn, etc. Oh dear, who can we trust to do it right!

Another thing to consider is whether your guests feel you are working too hard in the kitchen to prepare and serve a meal, and if so, does it make them uncomfortable. Remember, the guest is the most important part of the entire evening. Their ease and comfort should be first on your list.

The more you can prepare beforehand, the better. Organization and pre-preparation are key. Many of the recipes in this book can be prepped ahead of time – some the day before. Take advantage of this so that you can spend more time with your guests...that's why they are there – to enjoy!

Another tip is not to rush. Take time between the salad and main course. Allow more time between the main course and dessert. Enjoy dessert away from the table, if possible. Serve it in the living room where you can be comfortable and have relaxing conversation. Present dessert on a buffet table and let your guest serve themselves. Be creative, but make sure it is comfortable for them.

You know, we really haven't done much in life if we don't reproduce ourselves – if we don't share who we are and what we know with others, and if we don't pass on to friends and family and the next generation the gifts we have received. I have learned from my mother, my aunts, friends and family, and now from my daughters. All of these wonderful recipes are some of the ways they shared their lives with me. I hope they are of help and an encouragement as you step out and honor those wonderful people God puts in your path to bless. Enjoy!

Lynda

Brentwood Jewelry & Gifts

Brentwood Jewelry has been in the Brentwood community for over 35 years. Like The Puffy Muffin, we are one of the few companies that started with the same people who run our operation today. Both businesses have evolved and survived the

changes the city has gone through over the years. That is thanks to our customers.

With three generations of master craftsmen in manufacturing and jewelry repair, we are not an ordinary jewelry store. "Satisfied Customers Are Our Future" is our slogan and that's what we have created. When guests walk through our doors, friendly staff waits to greet them to a comfortable atmosphere. We care about our customers and the merchandise they purchase. Our customers are like our jewels – we make sure they are cared for. They always leave with an ongoing friendship and a business they know they can trust – whether it's for purchasing a special surprise, or cleaning and repair – it's just another way we're no ordinary jewelry store.

7012 Church Street • Brentwood, TN 37027

615-373-5959

Table of Contents

About the Artist
LASSIE MCDONALD CROWDER

Lassie McDonald Crowder in her studio, Nashville, Tennessee

Lassie McDonald Crowder has won numerous awards in local and regional shows including Central South, Nashville, Tennessee; Art With A Southern Drawl, Mobile, Alabama; Pennyroyal Exhibition, Hopkinsville, Kentucky; and Red Clay Survey, Atlanta, Georgia. She has also published in *The Artists Magazine*. Her paintings are included in numerous local collections, both private and corporate, including the Parthenon Permanent Collection, Nashville, Tennessee, and in national and international collections. In Nashville, she is represented by Local Color Gallery.

"I cannot remember a time when I did not draw or paint. I grew up outside of Murfreesboro where I learned to love the Middle Tennessee landscape. It was a natural step to paint it. I attended schools in Murfreesboro and received a degree in art from Middle Tennessee State University.

"The landscape remains my favorite subject. However, this all changed several years ago after I started to paint full time. I included three flower paintings in an all-landscape show. The response to these paintings was overwhelming and I realized how much color flowers added to my paintings. Soon thereafter, I received commissions for paintings of private homes and gardens.

"Second in enjoyment to painting is ferreting out scenes from which to paint. I trek about the countrysides in the United States and abroad to treasure hunt with my camera. I never know where I will find my next subject – a fine garden, a medieval village, or the next bend in the creek.

"My philosophy is quite simple, really. I see something that attracts me – a highlight, shadow, shape of an object, reflection in water, a rock wall, a sharp contrast of light and dark, or a striking color – and I plan in my mind how to reproduce it in paint. I paint almost every day and never tire of it."

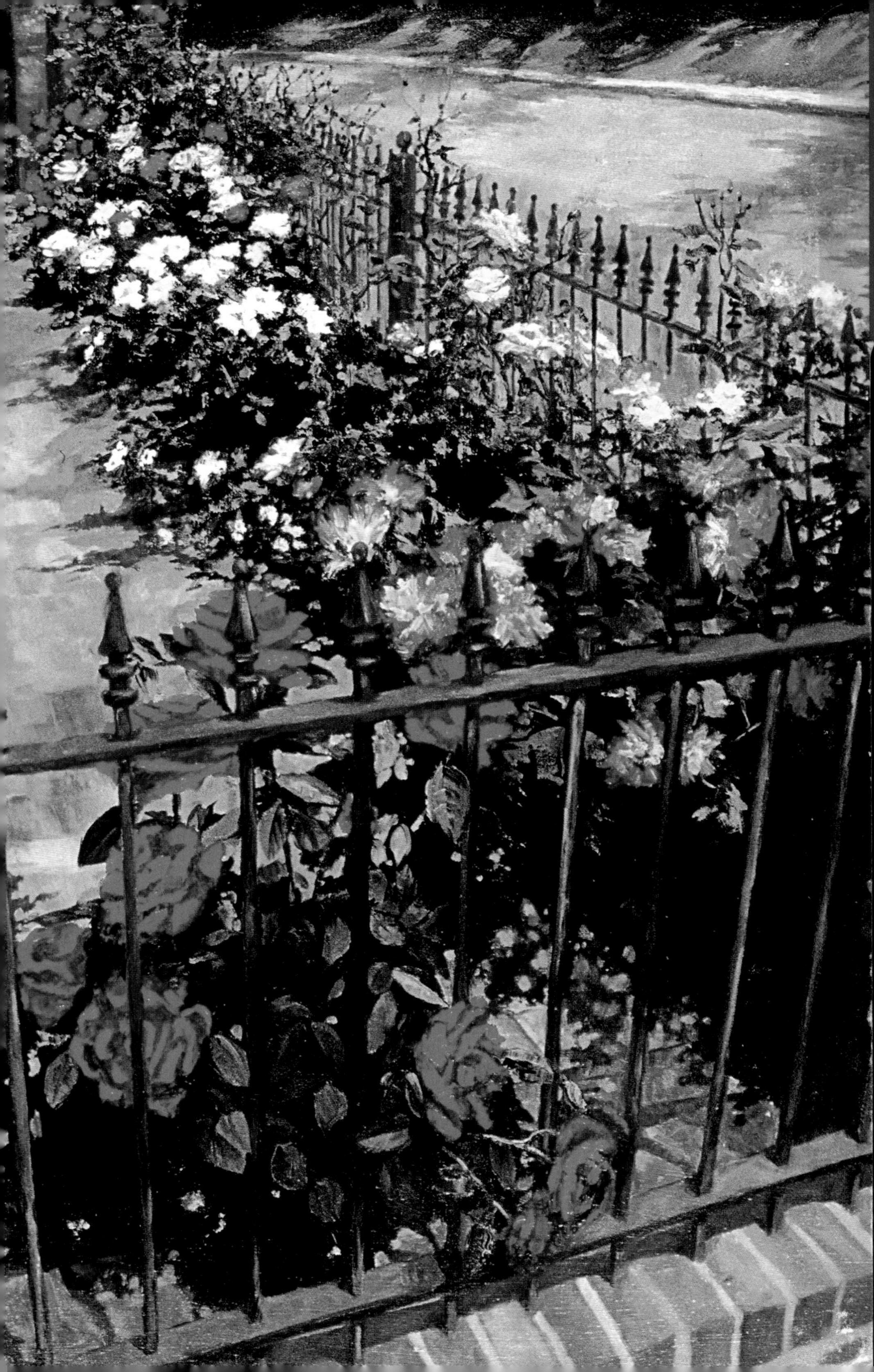

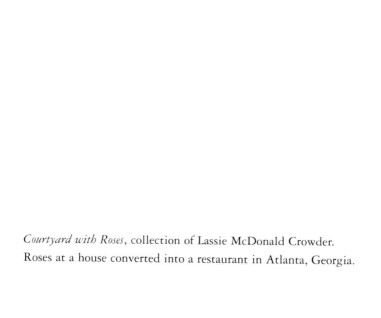

Courtyard with Roses, collection of Lassie McDonald Crowder.
Roses at a house converted into a restaurant in Atlanta, Georgia.

Basic Quiche

Quiche is a wonderful choice for breakfast, lunch or dinner – and it can be prepared many different ways with numerous combinations of flavors. All quiche recipes are essentially the same with a few variations. You can use heavy cream mixed with Purity Dairy milk, or mostly milk mixed with a little heavy cream. Using more cream will make the quiche dense in texture; mostly milk will make the quiche fluffier in texture. This is the recipe that we use at The Puffy Muffin.

5 Eggs, mixed with a fork

½ cup Half-and-Half

Salt & Pepper to taste

1½ cups Heavy Cream

1 Tbl. Flour mixed with ¼ cup Water

Combine all of the above ingredients and mix well with a wire whisk.

1 Deep Dish Pie Shell, uncooked

1 cup Cheese, shredded (Swiss, Cheddar, Muenster, Edam or any combination)

¼ cup or less Onion, finely diced

Herbs of choice

1 cup Ham or Bacon or Broccoli Florets or Asparagus or Mushrooms or Spinach – *your choice*

Sprinkle the cheese in the bottom of the pie shell. Next, layer the onions, herbs and any combination of main ingredients that you desire. You may want to add some mushrooms or peppers, or solely vegetables – be creative. Also, this is a good recipe with which to take advantage of your herb garden.

Pour the egg and cream mixture into the pie shell. Bake in a preheated 325° oven for 1 hour or until a knife inserted in the center comes out clean. Quiche should be served warm, so let your creation sit for 15 to 20 minutes after you take it out of the oven. Enjoy!

Pizza Quiche

A meat lover's delight!

Crust:

    Pepperoni slices

Filling:

    1 cup Ricotta Cheese

    3 Eggs, beaten

    4 ounces Italian Sausage, cooked, drained and cubed

    1 cup Mozzarella, shredded

    ½ cup Pepperoni, sliced and chopped

    ½ cup Cured Prosciutto or Ham, chopped

    ½ cup Hard Salami, chopped

    ¼ cup Parmesan Cheese, grated

Line a pie dish with pepperoni slices to form a crust.

Combine the remaining ingredients, mix well and pour into the crust. Bake in a preheated 350° oven for 30 to 45 minutes until the quiche is set and the edges are golden brown.

(Compliments of Alexandra Mattea, Pastry Chef, Dubrulle French Culinary School – Vancouver British Columbia)

Blueberry Muffins

1 cup Granulated Sugar

¾ cup Margarine

3 Eggs

3 cups Flour

5 tsp. Baking Powder

1 tsp. Salt

1 cup Purity Dairy Milk

1 cup Blueberries, drained

Cream the sugar and margarine. Add the eggs and the dry ingredients, alternating with milk. Fold in the blueberries. (This mixture can then be stored in the refrigerator for 2 to 3 weeks.) Let the batter stand in the refrigerator overnight. When ready to bake, stir the mixture well and pour into greased muffin tins. Bake in a preheated 375° oven for 20 minutes.

Breakfast Soufflé

This soufflé is scrumptious and an easy breakfast entrée that can be prepared ahead of time. Many thanks to my friend, Steph, for this recipe.

12 slices White Bread, ~~crusts removed~~ toasted + crumbled

1 to 1½ cups cooked Ham, chopped or Sausage, crumbled

2 cups Sharp Cheddar Cheese, shredded

5 ~~6~~ Eggs

3 cups Purity Dairy Whole Milk

½ to 1 tsp. Salt

1 tsp. dry mustard

Cut the bread into cubes and layer in a greased 9"x13" glass casserole dish. Next, layer the ham or sausage on top and sprinkle with cheese. Separately mix the eggs, milk and salt, and pour over the cheese layer. Refrigerate for 12 to 24 hours. Bake in a preheated 325° oven for 45 to 50 minutes.

last

(Compliments of my daughter Kristi Stone Elzinga)

Bran Muffins

3 cups All-Bran cereal

2 cups boiling Water

½ cup Vegetable Oil

2½ cups Flour

2½ tsp. Baking Soda

1 tsp. Salt

1½ cups Granulated Sugar

2 Eggs, beaten

2 cups Purity Dairy Buttermilk

Mix together the All-Bran, boiling water and oil. Allow the mixture to cool. Meanwhile, combine the flour, baking soda, salt and sugar. Set aside.

Mix together the eggs and buttermilk. Combine all of the mixtures and let the batter stand in the refrigerator overnight. (This mixture will keep for two weeks.) Pour the batter into greased muffin tins and bake in a preheated 400° oven for 20 minutes. Delicious!

(Compliments of my friend Beth Hutcheson)

Buttermilk Scones

4 cups Flour

1 Tbl. Baking Powder

1 tsp. Baking Soda

½ tsp. Salt

1 cup Granulated Sugar

6 ounces Butter, cut in pieces

1½ to 2 cups Raisins and/or Dried Cranberries and/or
    Dried Blueberries

1 cup Purity Dairy Buttermilk

1 Tbl. Vanilla Extract

Topping:

1 large Egg, beaten

1 cup Granulated Sugar and 1 Tbl. Cinnamon, mixed

Sift together the flour, baking powder, baking soda, salt and sugar into large a bowl. Add the butter pieces and blend with a pastry knife until the mixture resembles coarse meal. Mix in the raisins or dried berries. Add the buttermilk and vanilla. Stir with a wooden spoon and then by hand if necessary until the dough is sticky, but manageable.

Form the dough into a ball and transfer to a floured surface. Knead gently six times and then roll the dough out into ½" to 1" thickness. Using a 3" deep biscuit cutter, cut the dough into rounds and place on a baking sheet lined with waxed paper. Gently brush the scones with the egg and sprinkle with cinnamon sugar.

Bake in a preheated 300° oven for 18 to 20 minutes or until golden brown.

Caramel Pecan Rolls

Dough:

3 cups Bread Flour	1 cup Whole Wheat Flour
¼ cup Granulated Sugar	2 tsp. Salt
¼ ounce Instant Yeast (1 package)	½ cup Warm Water (110°)
1 cup Purity Dairy Milk, heated to room temperature	⅛ cup Vegetable Oil

Filling:

⅜ cup Butter, melted	⅜ cup Brown Sugar
1½ tsp.Cinnamon	½ cup Pecans, chopped

Glaze for bottom of pan:

¾ cup Brown Sugar	⅜ cup Butter
1½ Tbl. Light Corn Syrup	½ cup Pecans, chopped

Dough: Measure the dry ingredients into a mixing bowl. In a separate bowl, proof the yeast in the warm water. Set aside.

Heat the milk and add the oil to the milk. Combine the milk/oil with the dry ingredients. Add the proofed yeast. Mix well. Turn the dough out onto a lightly floured surface and knead until smooth and elastic in texture – about 5 minutes. Place the dough in a lightly oiled bowl and cover with a towel. Allow the dough to rise until doubled in bulk – about 1 hour. Place the dough on a floured surface and roll out to approximately 24"x8".

Filling: Brush the melted butter on the dough. Mix the brown sugar and cinnamon and sprinkle over the dough. Cover with the pecans. Roll the dough as you would a jelly roll, starting with the long edge. Pinch the dough to seal the edges. Cut the roll into 1" pieces with kitchen string or dental floss.

Glaze: In a sauce pan, combine the brown sugar, butter and corn syrup and warm over low heat, stirring constantly, until the mixture comes to a slow boil. Pour into the bottom of a 13"x9" pan. Sprinkle the pecans over the glaze in the pan. Place the rolls in the pan and allow to rise for 30 to 45 minutes.

Bake in a preheated 375° oven for 20 minutes. When done, invert so that the glaze is on the top of the rolls.

(Compliments of my sister Suzan Putman)

Oatmeal Raisin Scones

7 cups Flour

⅛ cup Baking Powder

1 Tbl. Baking Soda

2 tsp. Salt

1½ cups Granulated Sugar

1½ pounds Butter, cut in pieces

5½ cups Rolled Oats

2 cups Raisins

2½ cups Purity Dairy Buttermilk

Topping:

1 large Egg, beaten

½ cup Cinnamon & Sugar, mixed

Sift together the flour, baking powder, baking soda, salt and sugar into a large mixing bowl. Add the butter pieces and blend with a pastry knife until the mixture resembles coarse meal. Mix in the oats and raisins. Add the buttermilk and stir with a wooden spoon and then by hand if necessary until the dough is sticky, but manageable.

Form the dough into a ball and transfer to a floured surface. Knead the dough gently six times and then roll out into ½" to 1" thickness. Using a 3" deep biscuit cutter, cut the dough into rounds and place on a baking sheet lined with waxed paper. Gently brush the scones with the egg and sprinkle the tops with cinnamon sugar.

Bake in a preheated 300° oven for 18 to 20 minutes or until golden brown.

Chocolate Chip Banana Bread

1 ½ cups **Whole Wheat Flour**

2 tsp. **Baking Powder**

½ tsp. **Baking Soda**

⅛ tsp. **Salt**

½ cup **Brown Sugar**

2 **Eggs**

¼ cup **Purity Dairy Milk**

¼ cup **Vegetable Oil**

3 ripe **Bananas, mashed**

1 cup **Semi-Sweet Chocolate Chips**

½ cup **Walnuts, chopped** *(optional)*

½ tsp. **Vanilla**

Combine the flour, baking powder, baking soda, salt and brown sugar. Set aside.

In a separate bowl, mix together the eggs, milk and oil. Stir in the mashed bananas. Gradually stir in the flour mixture until moistened. Fold in the chocolate chips, walnuts and vanilla. Pour into one large or two small greased loaf pans. Bake in a preheated 350° oven for 45 minutes or until a knife inserted in the center comes out clean.

(Compliments of my daughter Kristi Stone Elzinga)

Hash-Brown Potato Casserole

(Serves 10)

3 pound bag Frozen Hash-Browns, thawed

1½ cups Cream of Chicken Soup

1½ cups Sour Cream

1 tsp. Salt

1 tsp. Pepper

Topping:

2 cups Cheddar Cheese, shredded

Potato Chips, crushed

Combine all of the ingredients and mix until moist, but not a soupy consistency. Top the casserole with the cheese and potato chips. Bake in a preheated 325° oven for 45 minutes.

Oven Omelet Brunch

¼ cup Butter

18 Eggs

1 cup Purity Dairy Milk

2 tsp. Salt

1 cup Sour Cream

¼ cup Green Onions, chopped

½ to 1 cup Cheddar Cheese

Melt the butter in a 13"x9" glass baking dish. In a large mixing bowl beat together the eggs, milk, salt and sour cream. Pour the mixture over the butter. Stir in the onions and top with cheese. Bake in a preheated 350° oven for 35 minutes or until the eggs are set, but moist.

Waffles

This is a delightful, light, turn-of-the-century recipe. Imagine your family's delight with "homemade" waffles. Definitely worth the effort and you may want to consider using real maple syrup!

2 Eggs, separated

2 Tbl. Granulated Sugar

1 tsp. Salt

2 Tbl. Butter, melted

2 cups Purity Dairy Milk

Flour to make thin batter (approximately 2 cups)

2 large tsp. Baking Powder

With wire whisk, beat together the egg yolks, sugar, salt, butter, milk and flour. Just before cooking, add the beaten egg whites and baking powder. Cook on a hot, greased waffle iron.

Yeast Biscuits

5 cups Flour, sifted *(If using Self-Rising Flour, eliminate the salt, baking soda and baking powder)*

2 Tbl. Granulated Sugar

1 tsp. Salt

1 tsp. Baking Soda

3 tsp. Baking Powder

1 cup Crisco

1 packet Dry Yeast, dissolved with ¼ cup warm water

2 cups Purity Dairy Buttermilk

Mix all of the dry ingredients. Cut the Crisco into the flour mixture. This should yield a crumbly consistency. Add the dissolved yeast and buttermilk. Blend well with a fork.

Roll out the dough and cut into biscuits. Place the biscuits on a greased cookie sheet and allow them to rise for 1 hour. Bake in a preheated 400° oven for 20 minutes.

Garden Chair, collection of Jim and Jane Harwell.
Chair and cottage in the garden at Sissinghurst Castle in Kent, England.

Sourdough Starter

½ cup Fennel Seeds

½ cup Caraway Seeds

½ cup Sesame Seeds

5 cups Flour

4 cups Water

Toast all of the seeds in a preheated 325° oven for 20 to 25 minutes. Allow the seeds to cool and then grind in a coffee grinder. With an electric mixer, mix the seeds with the remaining ingredients until well combined.

Place the mixture in a loosely covered container and allow it to ferment for 4 to 6 days. Small bubbles will appear on top of the starter to indicate it is ready to use. For continued use, feed the starter daily by mixing unused dough with 2 cups water and 2 cups flour.

(Compliments of Pastry Chef Sam Tucker)

Basic Sourdough Bread

2 cups Purity Dairy Buttermilk

3 ounces Instant Dry Yeast

3 tsp. Salt

2 Tbl. Olive Oil

2 cups Sourdough Starter (see page 26)

4 to 6 cups High Gluten or Bread Flour

Combine the buttermilk, yeast, salt, olive oil and the starter in an electric tabletop mixer with hook attachment. Gradually add the flour and mix on high speed until the mixture becomes elastic in texture and shiny. Let the dough rest, covered, for 1 hour in a warm place.

Roll out the dough on a flour-dusted work surface. Cut and form two 1-pound, 8-ounce loaves and roll into the desired shape. Be careful not to overwork the dough. Place any unused dough back into the starter. Allow the dough to rise, covered, at room temperature for 20 to 25 minutes. Bake in a preheated 450° oven for 35 to 40 minutes.

(Compliments of Pastry Chef Sam Tucker)

Pumpkin Bread

1 cup Pecan pieces

3½ cups Flour (½ cup reserved)

3 cups Granulated Sugar

2 tsp. Baking Soda

1 tsp. Salt

3 tsp. Cinnamon

1 tsp. Nutmeg

1 tsp. ground Cloves

¼ tsp. ground Ginger

4 Eggs

1 cup Vegetable Oil

½ cup Water

2 cups canned Pumpkin

1 cup Raisins, plumped

Combine the pecans with ½ cup of flour. When added to the batter, this process will keep the pecans from descending to the bottom of the bread while baking.

In a separate bowl, combine the remaining ingredients in the order listed. Beat with a mixer on medium speed. By hand, stir in the flour-coated pecans. Bake in two greased and floured loaf pans in a preheated 350° oven for 1 hour.

Butterhorn Rolls

½ cup Butter-Flavored Crisco

1 cup Purity Dairy Milk, scalded

½ cup Granulated Sugar

1 package Active Dry Yeast

1 tsp. Salt

3 Eggs, beaten

4 cups Flour

Butter, melted

Place the Crisco in a glass bowl and pour the scalded milk on top. When the mixture cools to lukewarm, add the sugar that has been premixed with the yeast. Stir with a whisk. Add the salt and eggs one at a time, whisking well after each addition. Slowly add the flour and mix with a large spoon.

Allow the dough to rise until doubled in size (about 1½ hours). Divide the dough into two pieces. Roll each into a 10" circle and brush with melted butter. As a pizza is sliced, cut the dough into 12 wedges. You should have 12 triangular pieces. Remove the pieces one at a time. Beginning at the wide end of the wedge, roll toward the pointed end until it curves into a crescent shape. Place each roll on a lightly greased baking sheet and let rise again until doubled in size. Bake the rolls in a preheated 350° oven for 8 to 10 minutes or until lightly browned. Brush with melted butter again.

(Compliments of employee Beverly Puckett)

Corn Bread Deluxe

1½ cups Self-Rising Cornmeal

½ to ⅔ cup Vegetable Oil

1 cup Sour Cream

1 cup Cream-Style Corn

2 Tbl. Onion, chopped

2 Eggs

1 tsp. Salt

Gently mix all of the ingredients by hand. The corn bread comes out best if it is poured into a greased, preheated iron skillet. This produces a nice crust on the edges. Bake in a preheated 350° oven for 30 minutes or until a knife inserted in the center comes out clean.

Corn Light Bread

2 cups Self-Rising Corn Meal

1 cup Flour

¾ cup Granulated Sugar

½ tsp. Salt

2¼ cups Purity Dairy Buttermilk

½ cup Vegetable Oil

Mix all of the ingredients with a wire whisk and pour into a greased loaf pan. Bake in a preheated 350° oven for 1 hour 10 minutes, or until a knife inserted in the center comes out clean.

Cherry Pecan Bread

2 cups Pecans

2 Tbl. and 1 tsp. Salt

2 cups Dried Cherries

1½ cups Orange Juice

2½ cups Sourdough Starter (see page 26)

1½ cups Water

½ cup Honey

3 ounces Instant Dry Yeast

6 to 8 cups High Gluten or Bread Flour

On a cookie sheet, toast the pecans in a preheated 350° oven for 20 minutes. Pour the pecans into a bowl and sprinkle with salt. Set aside to cool.

Plump the dried cherries in orange juice over low heat until they reach a simmer — or microwave for 3 minutes on high. Combine the starter, water, plumped and drained cherries, honey, yeast and half of the flour. Mix well and let the dough rise for an hour.

In an electric mixer or food processor, combine the cherry mixture with the remaining flour and toasted pecans. Mix until the dough is elastic in texture and shiny. Let the dough rest an additional hour.

Roll out the dough onto a flour-dusted surface. Cut the dough into four loaves. Gently knead and roll the dough into a rounded shape and place in a baking pan. Allow loaves to rise for 30 minutes at room temperature.

Bake in a preheated 350° oven for 30 to 35 minutes.

(Compliments of Pastry Chef Sam Tucker)

Native American Fry Bread

Indian Fry Bread is a traditional, every day part of the Native American meal. This recipe is one that my Great Grandmother and Grandma used. Our family get-togethers are not complete without the Fry Bread. Fourkillers and Cherokees everywhere value this recipe as one of our favorites.

½ tsp. Salt

½ tsp. Onion Powder *(optional)*

3½ cups Flour

1 cup warm Water

1 Egg, whisked

Vegetable Oil

Combine the salt, onion powder and 3 cups of the flour in a large bowl. Slowly add the warm water in small amounts and knead into the dough.

Slowly add the egg to the dough and knead into small portions. You may not use the entire egg. Knead the dough until it is soft, but not sticky. Use ½ cup flour as needed to keep the dough from becoming sticky. Cover the dough with a warm, damp cloth and let stand for 20 minutes.

Pull at the dough and form golf ball-size balls. Pat out the balls into thin rounds. In a heated cast iron skillet fry the dough in approximately 1" deep oil until golden brown. The bread is so light that it will float on the oil. The bread is ready to flip when bubbles appear. Flip the bread and fry until brown.

(Compliments of employee Kaela Fourkiller)

Poppy Seed Bread

3 cups Flour

2¼ cups Granulated Sugar

1½ tsp. Baking Powder

1½ tsp. Salt

3 Eggs

1½ cups Purity Dairy Milk

1½ cups Vegetable Oil

1½ Tbl. Poppy Seeds

1½ tsp. each of Vanilla, Almond, and Butter flavoring

Glaze:

¾ cup Granulated Sugar

¼ cup Orange Juice

½ tsp. Vanilla

½ tsp. Almond flavoring

½ tsp. Butter flavoring

Combine all of the main ingredients and beat for 2 minutes with a medium speed mixer. Bake in two large, greased loaf pans in a preheated 350° oven for 1 hour.

Glaze: Combine all of the glaze ingredients and mix well with a wire whisk. Pour over hot, just-out-of-the-oven bread.

Refrigerator Rolls

These rolls are great to have on hand in the freezer. Once the dough is formed into balls, it can then be frozen — ready for a short notice special meal. Before baking, simply allow the rolls to thaw for 2 hours and rise until doubled in size.

1 cup boiling Water

½ cup Granulated Sugar

1 tsp. Salt

½ to ⅔ cup Shortening

2 packages Yeast

1 cup lukewarm Water

6 cups Flour

2 Eggs

In a saucepan with the boiling water, add the sugar, salt and shortening. Allow the mixture to cool to room temperature.

Dissolve the yeast in the lukewarm water and add to the shortening mixture. Add 2 cups of the flour and the eggs and stir with a wire whisk until the mixture resembles pancake batter. Stir in the remaining 4 cups flour with a spoon. Allow the dough to sit, covered, in the refrigerator for 4 to 6 hours.

Form the dough into 1½" balls and place on a cookie sheet to let rise until doubled in size. Bake in a preheated 400° oven until lightly browned.

Cranberry Nut Loaf

4 cups Flour

2 cups Granulated Sugar

3 tsp. Baking Powder

2 tsp. Salt

1 tsp. Baking Soda

½ cup Vegetable Oil

1½ cups Orange Juice

2 Eggs

4 cups fresh Cranberries, washed, drained and chopped

1 cup Pecan pieces

Combine all of the ingredients except for the cranberries and pecans. Beat well to create a thick cake-like batter. Mix in the cranberries and pecans by hand. Pour the batter into two greased loaf pans. Bake in a preheated 350° oven for 1 hour.

Whole Wheat Bread

Absolutely delicious — hearty too!

1½ cups Potatoes, peeled and mashed

1 cup Granulated Sugar

1 cup Margarine

1 package Yeast, dissolved in 1 cup warm potato water

1 cup Purity Dairy Milk, scalded

1 tsp. Salt

2 Eggs, beaten

3 cups Whole Wheat Flour

In a saucepan with water that just covers the potatoes, cook the potatoes until tender. Reserve 1 cup of this potato liquid to dissolve the yeast. Mash the potatoes after draining.

Cream the sugar and margarine, and mix with the yeast, milk, salt and eggs. Cover and let rise until the mixture is doubled in size. Slowly add the flour and work the dough down in size. Knead the dough well and let it stand in the refrigerator overnight. Place the dough in greased loaf pans and allow it to rise until doubled in size. Bake in a preheated 350° oven for 30 minutes or until brown and firm on top.

(Compliments of my Aunt Mil)

Stream with Sycamores and Cedars, collection of Lassie McDonald Crowder.
A spring-fed stream near Livingston, Tennessee.

2 x 4 Soup

2 pounds Ground Chuck, browned and drained

2 (15-ounce) cans Rotel

2 (10-ounce) cans Small Kidney Beans

2 (19-ounce) cans Progresso Minestrone Soup

1 pound Velveeta Cheese

In a saucepan over medium-low heat, combine all of the ingredients and mix well. When the cheese melts the soup is ready to eat.

(Compliments of my Aunt Elva Scobey)

Baked Potato Soup

(Serves 8 to 10)

25 ounces Bechamel (white sauce), may be canned

25 ounces Cream of Chicken Soup, undiluted

½ pound Velveeta Cheese, cubed

½ cup Onion, chopped

1 quart Half-and-Half

Potatoes – amount desired, boiled with skins on, chopped

Pepper to taste

Combine the Bechamel and the Cream of Chicken soup in a heavy sauce pan. Heat over medium-low until the mixture begins to steam. Add the cheese and onions. As the cheese begins to melt, add the Half-and-Half. Heat this mixture until it begins to steam. Add the potatoes and pepper and stir well to incorporate the cheese. Serve and enjoy!

Burgundy Soup

(Yields 4 Quarts)

This recipe was provided with permission from Grace Episcopal Church in Anderson, S.C., by way of my daughter, Martha Scobey Hinson Booth. For one day each year the women hold a fundraiser for the Women of the Church. The ladies bring batches of this soup downtown where they sell a delightful lunch of the soup with cornbread and dessert. The project is always an overwhelming success!

1 pound Ground Beef

3 medium Onions, chopped

1 clove Garlic, minced

3 (10.5-ounce) cans double strength Beef Bouillon

2 (20-ounce) cans Tomatoes, chopped

1 cup Potatoes, diced in small pieces

1 cup Carrots, chopped

1 cup Celery, chopped

1 cup Green Beans – if canned, do not drain

***Optional:* Okra, Corn, Butter Beans**

1 cup or more Dry Burgundy Wine

2 Tbl. Parsley, freshly chopped or dried

½ tsp. Basil

¼ tsp. Thyme

1 cup Water

2¼ tsp. Salt or to taste

¼ tsp. Pepper or to taste

In a large frying pan, brown the beef, onions and garlic. Add the remaining ingredients and simmer for 90 minutes.

(Compliments of my Aunt Carolyn Scobey Hinson)

Beer Cheese Chowder

2 cups Potato, uncooked, finely diced

1½ cups Onion, diced

1 cup Carrots, grated

1 cup Celery, chopped

¼ cup Butter

6 Chicken Bouillon Cubes

2 cups Water

2 cups Purity Dairy Milk

½ cup Flour

4 cups Cheddar Cheese, shredded

1 tsp. Dry Mustard

Cayenne Pepper to taste

½ cup Beer

Parsley, chopped – *for garnish*

Place the potatoes, onions, carrots, celery, butter, bouillon cubes and water in a 4 quart sauce pan and bring to a boil. Reduce the heat and simmer for 30 minutes.

Combine the milk and flour with a whisk, and gradually blend into the vegetable mixture. Add the cheese, dry mustard and cayenne pepper. Simmer until the cheese melts. Stir in the beer and garnish with parsley.

Chicken Almond Soup

3 Chicken Breasts, with skin

1 cup Onion, chopped

1 cup Celery, chopped

1 cup Carrots, chopped

½ stick Butter

¾ cup Chicken Stock

4 Chicken Bouillon Cubes

1 cup White Wine

2 quarts Heavy Cream

1 cup Almonds

Boil the chicken breasts until cooked through. Reserve 1 cup of the broth from the water. Dice the chicken into bite-size pieces.

Sauté the vegetables in the butter. Add the chicken stock, bouillon cubes and diced chicken. Add the white wine, simmer for 2 minutes and then add the heavy cream. Bring the mixture to a boil and reduce to a simmer until the sauce thickens. The heavy cream will thicken the soup. Garnish with the almonds which can be toasted in butter.

(Compliments of former employee David Brown)

Chicken Enchilada Soup

This soup freezes very well. If it is too thick after being refrigerated or frozen, add chicken broth or Rotel.

3 Chicken Breasts, cut into thirds

2 to 3 Tbl. Canola Oil

½ to 1 Tbl. Onion Powder

Salt & Pepper to taste

½ cup Onion, chopped

½ tsp. Garlic Powder

1 cup Instant Corn Masa Flour

2 cups Water

2 (15-ounce) cans Chicken Broth

8 to 16 ounces Enchilada Red Sauce

1 tsp. salt

1 tsp. Chili Powder

½ tsp. Cumin

15 ounce can Corn, drained

15 ounce can Black Beans, rinsed and drained

10 ounce can Rotel Tomatoes

16 ounces Velveeta Cheese, cubed

Garnishes:

Tortilla Chips

Sour Cream

Sauté the chicken breasts in the oil over medium heat. Sprinkle the chicken with the onion powder, salt and pepper and cook until done. Remove the chicken and set aside to cool. Sauté the onion and garlic powder in the oil for 5 to 10 minutes. In a separate bowl, mix the masa flour with the water. Add the chicken broth, masa mixture, enchilada sauce, salt, chili powder, cumin, corn, black beans and Rotel tomatoes to the skillet. Shred the cooled chicken and add it to the mixture along with the cheese. At this point, the soup can slowly cook in a crock pot for several hours. To serve, garnish each bowl of soup with tortilla chips and sour cream.

(Compliments of Shani McMurtry)

Navy Bean Soup

(Serves 8 to 10)

This makes a wonderful meal on a cold winter's day. The anticipation grows throughout the day while the soup cooks and the aroma filters through the house. Serve this soup with corn muffins (see page 29).

1 pound bag Navy Pea Beans

6 cups Water, boiling

1 pound Ham Bone, cut in sections

2 tsp. Salt

1 cup Onion, chopped

2 medium Carrots, sliced thin

4 stalks Celery, chopped

1 large Potato, with skin, diced, uncooked

⅛ tsp. Dry Mustard

16 ounce can Tomato Puree

5 whole Cloves

10 Peppercorns

Salt & Pepper to taste

10 ounce can Rotel with diced tomatoes and green chilies

Rinse the beans thoroughly, removing any rocks or bruised beans. Pour the boiling water over the beans to 3" above the bean level. Soak for 12 hours.

The next day, drain the beans and place them in a soup pot with the ham bone. Add the salt and 6 cups of water. Bring to a boil and reduce the heat, simmering for 2 hours.

Add the remaining ingredients and simmer for 2 hours or until the beans are soft and the soup begins to thicken. Stir the soup occasionally to keep from scorching. Season with salt and pepper and if necessary, add water to desired consistency. Remove the ham bone and serve.

Yummy!

Southwest White Chili

(Yields 4 cups)

1 Tbl. Olive Oil

1½ pounds Chicken Breasts, boneless and skinless, cut into small
   cubes

¼ cup Onion, chopped

1 cup Chicken Broth

4 ounce can Chopped Green Chilies

1 tsp. Garlic Powder

⅛ tsp. Ground Red Pepper

1 tsp. Ground Cumin

½ tsp. Oregano Leaves

½ tsp. Cilantro

19 ounce can White Kidney Beans (Cannellini), undrained

Toppings:

2 Green Onions, sliced

Monterey Jack Cheese

Heat the oil in a large saucepan over medium-high heat. Add the
chicken and onions and cook for 4 to 5 minutes. Stir in the chicken
broth, green chilies and spices. Simmer for 15 minutes. Stir in the
beans and simmer for 5 more minutes. Top the chili with green onions
and Monterey Jack cheese if desired.

Black Bean & Beef Chili

(Yields 7 cups)

1 Tbl. Vegetable Oil

2 pounds Boneless Ground Chuck Beef, cut into ½" cubes

2 cups Onions, chopped

14.5 ounce can Beef Broth

1 cup Beer or Water

6 ounce can Tomato Paste

3 Tbl. Chili Powder

1 tsp. California Style Blend Garlic Powder

1 tsp. Oregano Leaves

½ tsp. Ground Cumin

½ tsp. Salt

2 (15-ounce) cans Black Beans, rinsed and drained

Heat the oil in a large saucepan over medium-high heat. Add the beef and brown. Drain off the oil. Add the onion and sauté for 5 minutes. Stir in the remaining ingredients except for the beans. Bring the chili to a boil. Reduce the heat and simmer for 1½ hours. Add the beans during the last 20 minutes of cooking.

Seafood Chowder

Beurre Manié:

   1 Tbl. Unsalted Butter, softened to room temperature

   4½ tsp. Flour

   1 Tbl. Butter, unsalted   1 Rib Celery, diced
   1½ cup sliced Leeks,   4 ounces Bacon, diced to ¼"
       white and light green   ⅔ cup Dry Vermouth
   2 cups Red Potatoes, diced   2 tsp. fresh Thyme
   2 cups Clam Juice or Fish Stock   1 cup Heavy Cream
   1 pound Shrimp, peeled,   Salt & Pepper to taste
       deveined, chopped and cooked   pinch of Cayenne

Make a beurre manié by mixing the butter with the flour. (This is an uncooked roux.) Set aside.

In a small pot of boiling water, blanch the bacon for 2 minutes to remove the excess fat and salt. Drain well.

In a medium stew pot, heat the butter and add the celery, leeks and bacon. Cook over medium heat until the leeks and celery turn bright green. Add the vermouth and bring to a boil until reduced by one-third.

Add the potatoes, thyme and clam juice or fish stock. Simmer until the potatoes are tender, but not mushy. Return the soup to a boil and whisk in the beurre manié a little at a time. Make sure there are no lumps. Pour in the cream and let the soup boil slowly. Add the shrimp and cook for 3 minutes. Turn off the heat and season with salt, pepper and cayenne.

* If desired, add a can of drained chopped clams, fresh clams, mussels in the shell, or a white fish such as tilapia – or you can make a corn chowder by using chicken stock instead of fish stock and then mix in 2 cups of fresh cut corn or canned corn that has been drained, using the corn juice as part of the stock.

(Compliments of my brother-in-law Gerry Putman)

Split Pea Soup

This is a fantastic recipe for the fall and a great use for the last of your tomato crop.

1 pound bag dry Split Peas	2 Ears Corn, must be fresh
8 cups Water	2 cups Onion, diced
2 cups Celery, diced with leaves	2 cups fresh Tomatoes, cubed
5 Whole Cloves	1 Tbl. Coarse Salt
Ground Pepper to taste	10 ounce can Rotel Tomatoes with Green Chilies *(optional)*

Soak the split peas overnight in hot water in a bowl large enough to accommodate twice the volume as the peas will swell while soaking.

With a sharp knife, scrape the kernels from the corn cob. After the kernels are removed, milk the cob by scraping the knife blade across the cob to obtain the juice.

Drain and rinse the peas and place them in a soup kettle with 8 cups of water. Bring the mixture to a rolling boil. Add the vegetables, cloves, salt and pepper and return to a rolling boil. Watch the pot to ensure the soup does not foam and run over. Reduce the heat to low and simmer for 2 hours. *Option:* After 2 hours, add the Rotel and simmer for 15 minutes.

For a thicker soup: In a separate bowl, combine 2 heaping Tbl. of flour and ½ cup water and mix to produce a paste without lumps. Slowly add the paste to the soup. Simmer for 15 minutes, stirring constantly to avoid scorching.

Taco Soup
(Yields 3½ Quarts)

1 pound Ground Chuck

1 large Onion, chopped

3 (15½-ounce) cans Mexican Style Chili Beans, undrained

15¼ ounce can Whole Kernel Corn, undrained

15 ounce can Tomato Sauce

14½ ounce can Whole Tomatoes, undrained and chopped

4½ ounce can Green Chili Peppers, chopped

1.25 ounce envelope Taco Seasoning Mix

1 ounce envelope Ranch Style Salad Dressing Mix

1½ cups Water

Toppings:

Corn Chips

Shredded Lettuce

Chopped Tomato

Sour Cream

Shredded Cheddar Cheese

Cook the beef and onion in a Dutch oven over medium-high heat until the meat is browned and the onion is tender, stirring until the meat crumbles. Drain the grease off the mixture.

Stir in the beans and the remaining ingredients and bring to a boil. Reduce the heat and simmer uncovered for 15 minutes stirring occasionally. Ladle the soup into bowls and serve with desired toppings.

(Compliments of my Aunt Elva Scobey)

Fresh Broccoli Salad

This salad is so fresh and delicious! Do not mix the dressing with the vegetables until ready to serve – and go light on the dressing.

Dressing:

- 1 cup Brown Sugar
- 1 cup Vegetable Oil
- ½ cup Apple Cider Vinegar
- 1 cup Ketchup
- 1 tsp. Salt
- ½ tsp. Pepper
- 1 tsp. Worcestershire Sauce

Salad:

- 6 cups Broccoli Florets, washed, drained, cut in bite-size pieces
- 2 cups Tomatoes, diced
- 1 cup Almonds, slivered
- ½ cup Onion, chopped

Toppings:

- 1 to 2 cups Cheddar Cheese, grated
- 10 slices Bacon, cooked and crumbled

Dressing: In a 1 quart jar combine all of the ingredients. Close the lid tightly and shake vigorously for 2 minutes. Any extra dressing may be stored in the same jar.

Combine the broccoli, tomatoes, almonds and onions. Gently toss with the desired amount of dressing, but make sure the salad is not too wet. Top the salad with cheese and bacon.

Broccoli Salad

Salad:

    4 to 5 cups fresh Broccoli, cut into pieces

    1 cup Raisins

    1 cup shelled Sunflower Seeds

    ¼ Red Onion, diced

    10 strips Bacon, cooked crisp and crumbled

Dressing:

    4 Tbl. Sugar

    1 Tbl. Apple Cider Vinegar

    ½ cup Miracle Whip Salad Dressing

Combine all of the salad ingredients in a large bowl. In a separate bowl, combine the dressing ingredients and pour over the salad. Gently toss and chill until ready to serve.

(Compliments of former employee Bonnie Yockman)

Buttermilk Salad

    15½ ounces Crushed Pineapple

    2 (3-ounce) packages Peach Jell-O

    1 cup Pecans, chopped

    2 cups Purity Dairy Buttermilk

    8 ounce carton Cool Whip

In a medium saucepan, heat the undrained pineapple until it reaches a boil. Add the Jell-O and dissolve, stirring well. Allow the mixture to cool and then add the buttermilk. Continue to cool and fold in the Cool Whip. Mix thoroughly and congeal in a 9"x13" pan.

(Compliments of my Aunt Elva Scobey)

Chive Potato Salad

A tasty, summer salad!

5 pounds Red Potatoes, cooked and cubed or sliced

2 tsp. Salt

½ tsp. Pepper

¾ cup Chives, chopped

1½ cup Sour Cream

½ to 1 cup Hellmann's Mayonnaise

2 Tbl. Brown Mustard

Combine the potatoes, salt, pepper and chives. Set aside.

Combine the sour cream, mayonnaise and mustard. With a spoon gently mix with the potato mixture – which should be moist. Allow the potato salad to chill for 4 hours so that the flavors combine and ripen. If the salad is dry, add extra sour cream.

Coleslaw

1 medium head Green Cabbage, chopped

1 cup Spinach Leaves, finely chopped

1 cup Carrots, finely chopped

1 cup Mayonnaise

1 Tbl. Granulated Sugar

2 tsp. White Vinegar

In a large bowl combine the cabbage, spinach and carrots. In a separate bowl mix the mayonnaise, sugar and vinegar until well blended. Pour this dressing over the cabbage mixture and toss well.

(Compliments of employee Fernando Rodriquez)

Corned Beef & Cabbage Salad

Although this recipe doesn't sound too appetizing, believe me — it's sensational! It's a good main course for a summer lunch.

Cabbage Layer:

1 envelope Gelatin	1 Tbl. Granulated Sugar
½ tsp. Salt	1¼ cup Water
2 Tbl. Lemon Juice	¼ cup Vinegar
2 cups Cabbage, finely shredded	2 Tbl. Green Pepper, finely chopped

Corn Beef Layer:

1 envelope Gelatin	½ cup Water
2 Tbl. Lemon Juice	¼ tsp. Salt
¾ cup Mayonnaise	¼ cup Onion, minced
½ cup Dill Pickle, chopped	½ cup Celery, diced
12 ounces Corned Beef	

Cabbage Layer: Mix the gelatin, sugar, salt and water in a pan over low heat. Heat and stir the mixture until the gelatin is completely dissolved. Add the lemon juice, vinegar, cabbage and pepper. Place the mixture in an 8" square glass dish and chill.

Corned Beef Layer: Mix the gelatin in the water and dissolve over low heat. Remove from the heat and add the lemon juice and salt. Allow to cool. Add the mayonnaise, onion, pickle, celery and corned beef. Pour the mixture over the top of the chilled and set cabbage layer. Chill for 4 hours. Cut into squares and serve.

Jamaican Rice

This is so good!

Salad:

    1 ½ cups Wild Rice, cooked

    2 Green Onions, chopped

    ¼ cup Red Onion, chopped

    ¾ cup Mandarin Oranges, drained

    ¾ cup Pineapple, drained, chopped

Dressing:

    ½ cup Red Wine Vinegar

    2 tsp. Dijon Mustard

    1 cup Olive Oil

    1 tsp. Granulated Sugar

    Salt & Pepper to taste

Chill the rice after cooking. Add the onions, oranges and pineapple to the chilled rice and toss gently.

Dressing: Mix all of the dressing ingredients well and add to the salad just before serving. Season with salt and pepper.

(Compliments of my daughter Kristi Stone Elzinga)

Marinated Vegetable Salad

This salad is a wonderful side dish for a summer meal and perfect when it is made the day before.

1 tsp. Salt
1 tsp. Pepper
¾ cup Cider Vinegar
½ cup Vegetable Oil
1 Tbl. Water
1 cup Granulated Sugar
16 ounce can Shoe Peg Corn, drained well
16 ounce can French Style Green Beans, drained well
16 ounce can LeSueur Peas, drained well
1 large Bell Pepper, chopped
3 to 4 Ribs Celery, chopped
1 Onion, chopped

Bring the salt, pepper, vinegar, oil, water and sugar to a boil. Boil for 2 minutes and set aside to cool.

Combine the remaining ingredients and toss with the cooled vinegar dressing. Chill the salad until ready to serve.

(Compliments of my friend Carol Boeing)

No Toss Salad

1 head Iceberg Lettuce, finely chopped

1 cup Celery, finely chopped

¼ cup Green Pepper, finely chopped

½ cup Onion, finely chopped

1 package frozen Green Peas, slightly cooked (3 minutes)

Garlic Salt

1 cup to 1 pint Hellmann's Mayonnaise

Toppings:

6 strips Bacon, cooked crisp and crumbled

2 Hard Boiled Eggs, grated

Layer the vegetables in a serving dish and lightly sprinkle with garlic salt. Spread the top layer with the mayonnaise. Cover tightly and refrigerate for 4 to 6 hours or overnight. Before serving, sprinkle the top with the bacon and grated eggs.

Waldorf Salad

¼ cup Heavy Cream

1 Tbl. Powdered Sugar

½ cup Mayonnaise

4 cups Red Apples, cubed

2 cups Fresh Pineapple, cubed

1 cup Celery, chopped

2 Tbl. Pecans, chopped – *for garnish*

Whip the heavy cream with the powdered sugar and then combine with the mayonnaise. In a large bowl, combine the apples, pineapple and celery. Lightly toss the fruit with the mayonnaise mixture to coat evenly. Garnish with the pecans.

(Compliments of employee Fernando Rodriquez)

Spinach Salad

Salad:

2 bunches fresh Baby Spinach

12 slices Bacon, cooked crisp and crumbled

2 Hard Boiled Eggs, shredded

1 cup fresh Mushrooms, sliced

Dressing:

2 Tbl. White Wine Vinegar

2 Tbl. fresh Lime Juice

⅓ cup Olive Oil

1 tsp. Salt

¼ tsp. Pepper

1 tsp. Granulated Sugar

1 tsp. Mustard

2 Garlic Cloves, minced

Garnish:

Mandarin Oranges

Red Onion, thinly sliced

Avocado, cut in wedges

Remove the spinach stems. Wash the spinach gently and pat dry with paper towels. Sprinkle the bacon, eggs and mushrooms over the top of the spinach.

Dressing: Combine all of the dressing ingredients and refrigerate for at least 4 hours.

Just before serving, gently toss the salad with the dressing. Garnish with mandarin oranges, onion and avocado.

(Compliments of my daughter Kristi Stone Elzinga)

Caesar Salad Dressing

1 Head Romain Lettuce

Dressing:

1 Tbl. Dijon Mustard

1 Tbl. Lemon Juice

1 Tbl. Worcestershire Sauce

Cracked Pepper to taste

Minced Garlic to taste

½ to 1 cup Olive Oil

½ cup Parmesan Cheese, finely grated

1 head Romaine Lettuce, washed and cut for salad

Toppings:

Croutons

Parmesan Cheese, shredded

Using a wire whisk, combine the mustard, lemon juice, Worcestershire, pepper and garlic. Slowly add the oil in a fine stream, whisking briskly for 2 minutes after the oil is completely incorporated. Add the parmesan cheese and chill.

Just before serving, in a large bowl toss the lettuce with a small amount of the dressing. The key is adding the right amount of dressing and not too much or your salad will be 'wet' and not lightly dressed.

Top the salad with additional parmesan cheese and croutons. Serve immediately.

Balsamic Dressing

1 cup Balsamic Vinegar
½ cup Spicy Brown Mustard
½ cup Honey
1 Tbl. Garlic, minced
2 cups Olive Oil
Salt & Pepper to taste

Combine the vinegar, mustard, honey and garlic with a wire whisk. In a fine stream, drizzle the olive oil into the mixture, combining with a wire whisk or hand mixer until the oil is incorporated. The mixture should be thick. If the oil is added slowly while being constantly mixed, the mixture should not separate. Add salt and pepper. Store the dressing in the refrigerator. This recipe can also be made in a food processor.

Honey Mustard Dressing

This dressing is wonderful with pork or on a salad. It is also the same mustard dressing that The Puffy Muffin uses on our sausage roll.

3 cups Spicy Brown Mustard
2 cups Mayonnaise
4 cups Powdered Sugar

Combine the mustard and mayonnaise in a mixing bowl. On medium speed, mix in the powdered sugar ½ cup at a time. When all of the powdered sugar is incorporated, the dressing should begin to thicken and is ready to use. This must be stored in the refrigerator.

Cranberry Congealed Salad

6 ounce box Lemon Jell-O

6 ounce box Raspberry Jell-O

2 cups Boiling Water

1 cup Crushed Pineapple, drained

16 ounce can Whole Cranberry Sauce

Poppy Seed Dressing:

1 cup Hellmann's Mayonnaise

1 Tbl. Poppy Seeds

Combine both Jell-O mixes with the boiling water and stir until dissolved. Stir in the remaining ingredients and mix well. Pour the mixture into a flat pan and refrigerate for 4 hours. Combine the dressing ingredients and refrigerate.

When ready to serve, cut the congealed salad into squares and top with a dollop of poppy seed dressing.

Frozen Cranberry Salad

(Serves 12)

2 (16-ounce) cans Whole Cranberry Sauce

16 ounce can Crushed Pineapple, drained

8 ounces Cream Cheese, softened

1 cup Pecans, chopped

1 cup Whipping Cream, sweetened with ¼ cup Granulated Sugar

Mix the cranberry sauce, pineapple, cream cheese and pecans until well incorporated. Whip the cream with the sugar and add to the cranberry mixture. Pour into a flat pan or individual molds and freeze.

Frozen Fruit Salad

Interesting — a congealed salad that is frozen.

16 ounce can Fruit Cocktail

2 (16-ounce) cans Sliced Peaches

16 ounce can Crushed Pineapple

2 small packages Lemon Jell-O

8 ounces Cream Cheese

1 pint Whipping Cream

Drain the fruit cocktail, peaches and pineapple, reserving all of the juices. Heat 2 cups of the juices to a boil and add the Jell-O. Remove from the heat and stir the mixture until the Jell-O completely dissolves.

Beat the cream cheese until smooth and add the Jell-O mixture. Separately, whip the whipping cream until stiff peaks form and then stir it into the fruit mixture.

Freeze the salad, stirring several times during freezing to prevent the fruit from settling at the bottom.

Frozen Strawberry Salad

(Serves 12)

24 ounces Cool Whip

1 to 2 pounds frozen Strawberries, with juice

1 pound can Crushed Pineapple, with juice

2 cups Mayonnaise

½ cup Granulated Sugar

Combine all of the ingredients and mix well. Pour into a 9"x13" Pyrex pan and freeze. Cut into squares and top with a dollop of mayonnaise and a cherry.

Lime Jell-O Salad

Tired of traditional, sweet Jell-O salads? Try this tasty surprise.

2 small boxes Lime Jell-O, dissolved in 1cup boiling water

1 cup Cottage Cheese

1 cup Hellmann's Mayonnaise (or less if desired)

1 Cucumber, grated

2 Tbl. Onion, chopped

Combine all of the ingredients and mix well. Pour into an 8" Pyrex mold and allow to congeal in the refrigerator for at least 3 hours.

Strawberry-Banana Congealed Salad

6 ounce box Strawberry Jell-O

2 cups Boiling Water

20 ounce package frozen Strawberries, partially thawed

8 ounce can Crushed Pineapple, including juice

2 large Bananas, sliced

½ cup Sour Cream, or more

In a mixing bowl dissolve the Jell-O in the boiling water. Add the strawberries, pineapple and bananas. Pour half the mixture into a square casserole dish and refrigerate until set. When it is set, smooth the chilled mixture with sour cream. Carefully pour the remaining half of the mixture on top of the sour cream and refrigerate the salad again until it is firmly set. You should have three layers.

(Compliments of my friend Carol Boeing)

Vera's Salad

This is a wonderful salad for spring and summer when you would rather not serve a sweet salad.

2 (3-ounce) boxes Lemon Jell-O, dissolved in 1½ cups boiling water

1 Avocado, grated

1 Cucumber, grated

4 ounce can Water Chestnuts, chopped

½ cup Onion or Green Onions, diced fine

2 cups Mayonnaise

Combine all of the ingredients and mix well. Chill for 4 hours or until ready to serve.

(Compliments of my Aunt Vera Scobey)

Homemade Pizza & Sauce

Please try this recipe – you won't believe the flavor!

Dough:

> **4 cups Flour**
>
> **2 packages Dry Yeast**
>
> **1 Tbl. Granulated Sugar**
>
> **1½ tsp. Salt**

Sauce:

> **6 ounce can Tomato Paste**
>
> **1¾ tomato paste can of Water**
>
> **Minced Garlic to taste**
>
> **Oregano to taste**
>
> **Salt & Pepper to taste**

Toppings as desired:

> **Onions**
>
> **Mushrooms**
>
> **Green Peppers**
>
> **Mozzarella Cheese**
>
> **Sausage (cooked and crumbled)**
>
> **Pepperoni, etc.**

Mix all of the dough ingredients with enough hot water to create a stiff dough. Cover and allow the dough to rise for 45 minutes. While the dough is rising, mix all of the sauce ingredients and simmer.

Grease and flour a pizza pan and place the dough on the pan to roll it out. Pour the pizza sauce over the dough to desired thickness. Add and arrange desired toppings, saving the cheese for the last 5 minutes of baking. Bake the pizza in a preheated 450° oven for 15 minutes. Remove from the oven and sprinkle with the cheese and bake for 5 additional minutes.

Puffy Muffin Chicken Salad

2 cups Chicken Tenders
½ cup Celery, chopped fine
½ to ⅔ cup Grapes, halved
Salt & Pepper to taste
½ to ⅔ cup Mayonnaise

Boil the chicken tenders in water until done. Drain and allow to cool. Pull, don't cut, the chicken into pieces and place in a mixing bowl. Add the celery, grapes, salt and pepper. Mix slightly. Stir in the mayonnaise with a fork or spoon. Adjust the flavor by adding more salt and pepper, and adjust the consistency by adding more mayonnaise. If this recipe is too 'wet' for your taste, omit some of the mayonnaise the next time you make the salad.

Puffy Muffin Pimento Cheese

This recipe is an approximation and depends on your taste preference. You may need to adjust the pimentos or the mayonnaise to satisfy your taste.

1 pound Velveeta Cheese, cut into cubes
3 cups Mayonnaise
2 cups Pimentos, drained but not dry
4 pounds Cheddar Cheese, shredded

Place the Velveeta in a mixer and with the arrow attachment, mix on medium speed while adding the mayonnaise $\frac{1}{4}$ cup at a time. When this mixture is incorporated, but not creamy, add the pimentos. Continue mixing and add the cheddar cheese a handful at a time. When all of the cheese is incorporated, your spread is done. Be careful not to mix beyond this point. This spread must be kept in the refrigerator.

Boats, Venice, collection of Angelyn Jenkins Smith.
A quiet canal at noon in Venice, Italy.

Baked Chicken Supreme

2 cups Sour Cream

¼ cup Lemon Juice

4 tsp. Worcestershire Sauce

4 tsp. Celery Salt

2 tsp. Paprika

4 Garlic Cloves, minced

3 tsp. Salt

½ tsp. Pepper

6 whole Chicken Breasts, halved to make 12 pieces

1¾ cup Potato Chip crumbs

Combine the sour cream, lemon juice, Worcestershire, celery salt, paprika, garlic, salt and pepper. Place the chicken in the mixture to coat well. Cover and refrigerate overnight.

Roll the chicken in the potato chip crumbs and place in a shallow baking dish. Cover with aluminum foil and bake in a preheated 375° oven for 30 minutes. If the chicken breasts look dry, drizzle with a small amount of melted butter. Bake an additional 30 minutes uncovered.

Chicken Tetrazzini

12 ounces Spaghetti

1 Tbl. Vegetable Oil

1 tsp. Salt

1½ Tbl. Butter

¼ cup Onions, chopped

2 Tbl. fresh Parsley, chopped

2 Tbl. Red Bell Pepper, diced

2 cans Cream of Mushroom Soup

1 cup Chicken Broth

3 cups Velveeta Cheese, shredded

4 cups Chicken, cooked and diced

In boiling water, cook the spaghetti adding oil and salt until al dente. Drain well.

In a large saucepan melt the butter and add the onions, parsley, bell pepper, soup, broth, salt and ½ cup of cheese. Add the spaghetti and chicken. Stir well. Transfer the mixture to a Pyrex dish and top with the remaining cheese. Bake uncovered in a preheated 350° oven for 30 to 45 minutes.

(Compliments of employee Fernando Rodriquez)

Chicken and Yellow Rice

Prepare the rice for this dish the day before serving. It's a wonderful entrée for a crowd.

4 or 5 Chicken Breasts

1-pound, 12-ounce can Whole Tomatoes, chopped into large pieces

3 to 4 tsp. Vegetable Oil

2 medium Onions, chopped

2 Garlic Cloves, chopped

2 medium Green Peppers, chopped

2 cups Long Grain Rice (soak in water overnight, drain the next morning)

2 Bay Leaves

2 cups Chicken Broth (reserved water from boiling the chicken)

3 cups Water

2 tsp. Turmeric

Boil the chicken until tender. Remove from the bone and chop into bite-size pieces. Place the chicken in a large roaster and layer the tomatoes over the chicken.

Sauté the onions, garlic and peppers in oil until soft. Distribute evenly over the tomatoes.

Next, add the rice and bay leaves. Pour the chicken broth mixed with the water and turmeric over the entire casserole. Bake in a preheated 400° to 425° oven for 30 minutes. Reduce the heat to 375°, cover with foil and cook for approximately 1 hour until the rice is cooked.

Chicken Enchiladas

5 Tbl. Butter

¾ cup Onion, chopped

½ cup Green Pepper, chopped

2 cups Chicken, cooked and shredded

¼ cup Flour

1 tsp. Coriander

½ tsp. Salt

3 cups Chicken Broth

1 cup Sour Cream

1½ cups Cheddar & Monterey Jack Cheeses, shredded

10 Flour Tortillas

Toppings:

Jalapeño Peppers, chopped

Fresh Tomatoes, chopped

Sauté the onion and pepper in 2 Tbl. butter. Add the chicken, combine well and set aside.

Using the same skillet, melt 3 Tbl. butter and blend in the flour, coriander and salt. Whisk in 2½ cups chicken broth and cook until thick and bubbly. Remove from the heat and add the sour cream and ½ cup cheese. Stir half of this sauce into the chicken mixture. Spoon a small amount of the sauce on both sides of the tortilla and fill with ¼ cup of the chicken mixture. Roll the tortillas and place in a casserole dish, seam side down.

Mix ½ cup chicken broth with the remaining sauce and pour over the enchiladas. Sprinkle with the remaining cheese and bake, uncovered in a preheated 350° oven for 30 minutes. Sprinkle jalapeños and tomatoes on top just before serving.

(Compliments of my daughter Kristi Stone Elzinga)

Enchilada Casserole

Delicious!

2 cups Chicken, cooked and shredded

4.5 ounce can Green Mexican Chilies

6 ounce can Salsa Verdé (green sauce)

½ tsp. Chicken Bouillon

2 cups Heavy Cream

12 small Corn Tortillas

1½ cup Monterey Jack Cheese, shredded

In a small bowl combine the chicken, chilies and salsa. Separately, combine the bouillon and heavy cream with a whisk. Fry or microwave the tortillas until soft. Cover with Saran Wrap to keep warm and soft as you prepare the casserole.

Dip each tortilla in the cream sauce and place several spoonfuls of the chicken mixture in the center. Roll the tortillas and place in a baking dish. Pour the remaining cream sauce over the top of tortillas and sprinkle with cheese. Cook uncovered in a preheated 350° oven for 30 minutes.

Jane's Chicken

This dish can be assembled ahead of serving and frozen for baking later.

6 Boneless Chicken Breast Halves

2 Eggs, salted and beaten

Italian Breadcrumbs

½ stick Butter

7 ounce can Mushrooms, sliced

¼ pound Muenster Cheese

Cut the chicken into bite-size pieces and soak in the egg wash for 30 minutes. After soaking, roll the chicken bites one at a time in a bowl filled with breadcrumbs.

Melt the butter in a skillet and sauté the chicken until it turns golden brown. Place the chicken pieces in a greased casserole dish and top with mushrooms, including juice. Top with sliced cheese and bake, uncovered, in a preheated 350° oven for 30 minutes.

Sour Cream Chicken

3 to 4 cups Fritos, slightly crumbled

3 cups Chicken, cooked and shredded

1 cup Green Chilies

½ cup Onion, chopped

2 cups Cheddar or Monterey Jack Cheese

½ tsp. Salt

½ tsp. Pepper

1½ cups Sour Cream

In a greased 11"x9" pan, alternate layers of Fritos, chicken, chilies, onions, cheese and sour cream. Cover and bake in a preheated 325° oven for 30 minutes. Uncover, add some reserved Fritos and bake an additional 10 minutes.

Italian Chicken Breasts

8 Chicken Breast Halves, boneless and skinless

Vegetable Oil, to cover skillet ⅛" deep

Breading:

1 pound Mozzarella Cheese, shredded

2 cups Flour

½ cup Dried Parsley Flakes

⅓ cup Parmesan Cheese, shredded

1 package Dry Italian Dressing Mix

Milk Bath:

1 cup Purity Dairy Milk

2 extra large Eggs

1 cup Flour

In a bowl, mix together the breading ingredients. Set aside. In a separate bowl whisk together the ingredients for the milk bath.

Coat the chicken with the breading mixture; dip the coated chicken into the milk bath; and lastly dip again into the breading mixture. Heat the oil ⅛" deep in a skillet over medium heat. Add the chicken and cook for 5 to 6 minutes on each side.

(Compliments of employee Fernando Rodriquez)

Jerusalem Artichoke Chicken

(Serves 4)

Rice is the perfect accompaniment to this dish.

1 cup plus 2 Tbl. Flour

1 tsp. Garlic Salt

1 tsp. dried Dill

8 Chicken Breast Halves

¼ cup Vegetable Oil

2 Tbl. Butter

2 to 3 cups Half-and-Half

1 Tbl. Dijon Mustard

16 ounce can Artichoke Hearts, drained and quartered

Combine 1 cup of the flour with the garlic salt and dill. Dredge the chicken breasts in the seasoned flour.

In a skillet, heat the oil and fry the chicken on both sides until golden brown – about 15 minutes. Remove the chicken and keep warm. Pour off the oil, reserving the crusty particles in the bottom of the skillet. Add the butter and the remaining 2 Tbl. flour to the pan. Stir and cook over medium heat until smooth and bubbly. Slowly add the Half-and-Half until the mixture is the consistency of pancake batter. Add the mustard and artichokes hearts. When the sauce is heated through and thickened, pour it over the chicken and serve.

(Compliments of Dale Shearin, our angel)

Creamed Chicken on Cornbread

This is a very old recipe and too good! Most families have a form of this wonderful dish, this is mine. It is very rich, but if enjoyed on special occasions, it won,t add too much to your waistline!

½ stick Butter

⅔ cup Onions, chopped

⅔ cup Celery, sliced

3 Tbl. Flour

1 cup Purity Dairy Milk

1½ cups Half-and-Half

Salt & Pepper to taste

1 to 1½ cups Chicken, cooked and shredded

½ cup Carrots, shredded

½ to ⅔ cup Frozen Peas

1 to 2 Tbl. Cognac or Brandy

In a large skillet over medium heat, sauté the onions and celery in the butter. Stir in the flour and milk to create a roux. Slowly add the Half-and-Half and salt and pepper. Fold in the chicken, carrots and peas and cook for only a few minutes until the mixture thickens. Lastly, add the Cognac or Brandy.

If the creamed chicken becomes too thick, you may add heavy cream a tablespoon at a time. After the mixture thickens to desired consistency, let it sit overnight in the refrigerator to allow the flavors to ripen.

When ready to serve, reheat the creamed chicken over very low heat. If still too thick, add heavy cream just before serving. Serve over sliced cornbread squares (see recipe page 30).

Beef Brisket

4 pound Beef Brisket

4 ounce bottle Liquid Smoke

½ tsp. each: Onion Salt, Celery Salt and Garlic Salt

5 ounce bottle Worcestershire Sauce

6 ounces Barbeque Sauce

Tightly wrap the brisket in heavy duty aluminum foil and place in a baking dish – fat side up. Open the foil and pour the liquid smoke over the brisket. Sprinkle with the onion, celery and garlic salt. Tightly close the foil and refrigerate overnight.

Open the foil and drain off the liquid smoke. Cover the brisket with half the bottle of Worcestershire. Tightly close the foil and bake in a preheated 275° oven for 5 hours. Unwrap and add the barbecue sauce. Return to the oven for 1 hour, uncovered. Slice the brisket diagonally across the grain.

(Compliments of my Aunt Elva Scobey)

Marinated Pork Tenderloin

2 to 3 pounds Pork Tenderloin

2 cups Soy Sauce

½ cup Red Wine Vinegar

1 cup Brown Sugar

1 Tbl. Garlic, minced

1 tsp. Pepper

8 ounce can Crushed Pineapple, with juice

Place the tenderloin in a baking dish and set aside. Combine the remaining ingredients and mix well. Pour the mixture over the tenderloin and refrigerate for 1 to 2 hours.

Drain off all of the marinade and bake in a preheated 375° oven for 25 to 30 minutes or until a meat thermometer reaches 165°. Slice and serve.

(Compliments of Jason Burns, General Manager)

Bulgogie

This is undeniably yummy! It's even good cold the next day – should there be any leftovers! This dish makes a beautiful presentation on a platter with the onions to one side of the meat.

3 pounds Lean Beef (Sirloin Tip Roast)
1 large Onion, cut into ¼" to ½" slices, separating slices into rings

Marinade:

1 cup Vegetable Oil
¼ cup Granulated Sugar
5 ounces Soy Sauce
2 tsp. Garlic, minced
½ tsp. Salt
1 tsp. Pepper
6 Tbl. Sesame Seeds

Cut the roast into French fry-sized strips.

Marinade: Combine the marinade ingredients and whisk briskly. Marinate the meat and onions overnight.

Cover a grill rack with aluminum foil and punch holes in the foil all over. Layer the roast strips on the foil and grill on a high fire until medium rare, flipping to ensure even cooking. Usually this process takes only one flip, as you will place each piece of beef individually on the grill. By the time you get each strip placed, it will be time to start flipping the slices to the other side. After the meat is done and removed from the grill, place the onions all at once on the hot grill that is still covered with foil. Sauté until tender.

(Compliments of my friend Beth Hutcheson)

Beef Burritos

(Serves 5 to 6)

1 pound Ground Beef

¼ cup Onions, chopped

¼ cup Green Pepper, chopped

¼ cup Celery, chopped

1 pound can Refried Beans

½ to 1 cup Ketchup

1 to 2 Jalapeño Peppers, chopped

8 ounce can Mushrooms, drained or fresh

1 package large Flour Tortillas

8 to 16 ounces Hot Enchilada Sauce

Toppings:

2 cups Cheddar or Monterey Jack Cheese (or combination), grated

4 ounce jar Jalapeño Relish

Fry the ground beef with the onion, green pepper and celery. Drain well and mix with the beans, ketchup, peppers and mushrooms. Set aside.

Heat the tortillas in the microwave until just warm. For easy handling, cut the top off of the package and heat the tortillas in the original packaging.

Spoon a small amount of the beef mixture onto each tortilla and roll it up. Spoon additional mixture and enchilada sauce on top. Sprinkle with cheese and bake in a preheated 350° oven for 20 minutes. Remove from the oven and top with jalapeño relish.

Kielbasa &
Hot German Potato Salad Dinner

9 medium White Potatoes

6 slices Bacon

¾ cup Onion, chopped

2 Tbl. Flour

2 Tbl. Granulated Sugar

2 tsp. Salt

½ tsp. Celery Seed

Pepper to taste

¾ cup Water

⅓ cup White Vinegar or Cider Vinegar

2 (1-pound) packages Kielbasa

2 Tbl. Shortening

Clean the potatoes and boil in salted water until tender. Drain and when cooled, thinly slice. Set aside.

In a large skillet fry the bacon until crisp. Remove the bacon and in the bacon drippings, stir in the onions and cook until golden brown. Blend in the flour, sugar, salt, celery seed and pepper. Stir well and cook over low heat until the mixture is bubbly. Stir in the water and vinegar and heat to a boil, stirring constantly. Add the bacon and potatoes to the hot mixture and heat well, stirring to coat the potatoes.

In a separate skillet, brown the Kielbasa on all sides in the shortening. Serve with the potato salad.

(Compliments of Marcy Batterton, Front-End Manager)

Martha's Company Casserole

So easy, but a pleasant surprise.

4 cups (12-ounce bag) Egg Noodles

1 Tbl. Butter

1 pound Ground Beef

2 (8-ounce) cans Tomato Sauce

1 cup Cottage Cheese

8 ounces Cream Cheese, softened

¼ cup Sour Cream

⅓ cup Scallions, minced

1 Tbl. Green Pepper, minced

2 Tbl. Butter, melted

Cook the noodles according to package directions. Drain well.

Sauté the ground beef in the butter until brown. Stir in the tomato sauce and remove from the heat. In a separate bowl combine the cottage cheese, cream cheese, sour cream, scallions and green pepper.

In a 2 quart casserole dish, layer half of the noodles, then the cheese mixture and remaining noodles. Top with the melted butter and tomato sauce mixture. Refrigerate for 1 hour. Bake in a preheated 375° oven for 45 minutes.

Sausage Casserole

2 pounds Hot Sausage

2 medium Onions, chopped

1 Green Pepper, chopped

1 Rib Celery, chopped

2 cups White Rice, uncooked, but not Minute Rice

3 packages Lipton Dehydrated Chicken Noodle Soup

3 ounces Slivered Almonds

½ cup or less Soy Sauce

Fry the sausage in a skillet. Remove the meat and sauté the onions, green pepper and celery. Drain well.

In a saucepan, add the rice and dry soup mix to 8 cups boiling water. Reduce the heat, cover, and cook slowly for 30 minutes.

Combine both mixtures and add the almonds and soy sauce. Mix well and place in a casserole dish. Bake in a preheated 325° oven for 30 minutes.

Meat Loaf

1 pound Ground Beef

⅓ cup Oatmeal

½ Onion, diced

¼ cup Red Bell Pepper, diced

¼ cup Chili Sauce or Ketchup

⅛ cup Purity Dairy Milk

1 Egg

¾ tsp. Salt

½ tsp. Pepper

2 Tbl. Ground Horseradish *(optional)*

Glaze:

¼ cup Ketchup

2 Tbl. Brown Sugar

2 tsp. Dry Mustard

Combine all of the main ingredients in a large bowl and mix well by hand. The mixture should be just firm enough to hold a loaf shape. Place the mixture in an oven proof pan and shape the loaf.

Glaze: Combine all of the glaze ingredients and mix well. Cover the meat loaf with half of the glaze and bake in a preheated 350° oven for 30 minutes. Glaze the meat loaf again and cook an additional 15 minutes. With a meat thermometer, check for an internal temperature of 155°. Remove the meat loaf from the oven and allow it to rest for 10 minutes before slicing.

(Compliments of my brother-in-law Gerry Putman)

Spaghetti Sauce

This sauce is one of my family's favorites — absolutely delicious! This recipe makes enough for two meals for a family of four. It freezes very well, but may need to be thickened after thawing.

1 pound Lean Ground Beef

1 pound Ground Pork or Sausage

⅔ cup Onion, chopped

2 Cloves Garlic, crushed

2 (6-ounce) cans Tomato Paste

15 ounce can Tomato Sauce

28 ounce can Diced Tomatoes

10 ounce can Rotel Diced Tomatoes with Green Chilies

1 Tbl. Crushed Oregano

1 tsp. Basil

½ cup Ketchup

1 Tbl. Worcestershire Sauce

2 tsp. Kosher Salt

½ cup Black Olives, sliced

1 cup Mushrooms, sliced

In a large pan, brown the beef and pork. Remove the meat and drain off the excess fat. Place the meat mixture in another bowl and set aside. In the same pan, sauté the onions and garlic until just tender. Return the meat to the pan with the onions. As the meat and onions gently simmer, add both cans of tomato paste. Fill each of the tomato paste cans with water and add to the meat. Make sure to empty all of the tomato paste from the can. Mix well. The mixture should be very thick.

Next, add the tomato sauce, diced tomatoes and Rotel. Stir well and add the herbs, Ketchup and Worcestershire. Add the salt and simmer for 2 hours or until the sauce thickens. Leave the top on the pan slightly ajar to allow steam to escape, allowing the sauce to thicken quicker. During the last 30 minutes, add the olives and mushrooms. If the sauce is not thick enough, combine 1 Tbl. cornstarch with ½ cup cold water and add to the sauce while it is simmering.

Hot Sauce

This is a perfect sauce for barbeque.

¼ pound Butter, melted

½ pint Ketchup

½ pint Apple Cider Vinegar

½ Tbl. Tobassco

2.5 ounces Worcestershire Sauce

½ Tbl. Brown Sugar

1 Tbl. Onion, chopped

1 Garlic Clove, finely chopped

2 Tbl. Salt

With a wire whisk, combine all of the ingredients. Stir until the sauce is well combined.

Barbecue Shrimp

This is scrumptious when served with crusty French bread — and you'll be missing out if you don't dip the bread in the flavorful sauce.

½ tsp. Cayenne

½ tsp. Pepper

1 tsp. Garlic Powder

1 tsp. Salt

½ cup Butter

⅛ tsp. Tabasco Sauce

¼ cup Worcestershire Sauce

juice of 1 Lemon

1 ½ pounds Shrimp, unpeeled

Combine the dry ingredients and sprinkle evenly over the shrimp, stirring well to coat. In a saucepan, combine the butter, Tabasco, Worcestershire, and lemon juice and warm over low heat until the butter melts. Add this mixture to the shrimp and stir well. Pour the shrimp in a single layer in a baking dish and bake in a preheated 350° oven for 20 minutes.

(Compliments of my brother-in-law Gerry Putman)

Seafood Pasta

8 ounces Linguini or favorite pasta

3 Tbl. Butter or Margarine

1 Tbl. Garlic, minced

¼ cup Red Pepper, diced

pinch of Salt

½ tsp. Paprika

pinch of Cayenne Pepper

8 to 10 ounces Shrimp, peeled and deveined

1 cup Heavy Cream

¼ cup Parmesan Cheese

Cook the pasta according to package directions. In a large skillet combine the butter, garlic, diced peppers, salt, paprika, cayenne and shrimp. Sauté until the shrimp are pink and firm. Reduce to medium heat. Add the cream and parmesan cheese, stirring constantly. When the cream becomes thick and bubbly, pour it over the pasta and serve.

(Compliments of Jason Burns, General Manager)

Gertie's Crab Cakes

1 Egg

2 Tbl. Mayonnaise

1 tsp. Dry Mustard (or Dijon)

½ tsp. Pepper, freshly ground

1 tsp. Old Bay Seasoning

2 tsp. Worcestershire Sauce

dash of Tabasco Sauce

Cayenne to taste *(optional)*

1 pound Lump or Backfin Crabmeat, picked

⅓ cup Breadcrumbs

¼ cup Red Pepper and Onion, finely diced

Salt to taste

In a bowl, combine the egg, mayonnaise, mustard, pepper, Old Bay, Worcestershire, Tabasco and cayenne and mix well.

Place the crabmeat in a separate bowl and sprinkle with breadcrumbs. Pour the egg mixture over the crab and add the red pepper, onion and salt. Gently fold the ingredients together, careful not to break the lumps of crab. Form the cakes by hand into 8 mounds about 3" in diameter and ¾" thick. Do not pack the mixture – the cakes should be only as tight as necessary to stay together.

Place the cakes on a plate lined with wax paper, cover and refrigerate at least 1 hour.

Preheat a sauté pan and add a small amount of clarified butter. Cook the cakes turning several times until brown on both sides – about 8 total minutes.

(Compliments of my brother-in-law Gerry Putman)

Crab Cakes with Rémoulade

1 **Red Pepper, diced fine**   3 **Yellow Peppers, diced fine**

8 **scallions, thinly sliced**   4 **Tbl. Dill**

4 **tsp. fresh Garlic, minced**   2 **Tbl. Salt**

2 **Tbl. Coarse Ground Pepper**   8 **pounds Crab, steamed and
                                         drained well**
2 **cups Mayonnaise**
                                      ½ **cup fresh Breadcrumbs**
8 **Eggs, lightly beaten**

Vegetable oil – *for frying*

Combine the red and yellow peppers, scallions, dill, garlic, salt and pepper. Add the mixture to the crab and stir well. Add the mayonnaise and eggs and mix thoroughly. Add the breadcrumbs to desired consistency and combine thoroughly.

Shape the mixture into 2" cakes and shallow fry in oil for 4 minutes per side. Serve with the rémoulade.

Rémoulade:

1 **cup Whole Grain Mustard**   1 **cup Dijon Mustard**

1 **cup Mayonnaise**   ½ **cup Sweet or Dill Relish
                                         (if using dill relish,
3 **Tbl. Capers**   omit the dill weed below)**

Tabasco, Cayenne and Paprika,   1 **Tbl. Chervil**
    to taste
                                      1 **Tbl. Lemon Juice**
½ **Tbl. Dill Weed**

1 **Tbl. Rice Wine Vinegar or
    White Balsamic Vinegar**

Combine all of the ingredients and mix well. Refrigerate and serve with crab cakes. This is very spicy and full of flavor.

*(Compliments of Jason Valentine, Chef,
Johnson and Wales)*

Authentic Shrimp Etouffee

(Serves 6 to 8)

This dish is extra delicious when made a day before serving.

1½ stick Butter	¼ cup Flour
1 cup White Wine with 1 cup Water	1 Bay Leaf
⅛ tsp. Thyme	1 tsp. Basil
1 cup Green Onion, chopped	1 cup Yellow Onion, chopped
2 cloves Garlic, minced	½ cup Green Pepper
½ cup Celery, chopped	8 ounce can Tomato Sauce
2 tsp. Salt	1 Tbl. Worcestershire Sauce
½ tsp. Pepper	Tabasco Sauce to taste
2 pounds Shrimp, peeled and deveined	1 Tbl. Lemon Juice
¼ cup Fresh Parsley	1 Tbl. Lemon Rind, grated
	White Rice

Make a caramel-colored roux by simmering the butter and flour, stirring constantly. Add the wine mixed with the water, bay leaf, thyme, basil, green onion, yellow onion, garlic, green pepper and celery. Sauté for 30 minutes.

Stir in the tomato sauce, salt, Worcestershire, pepper and Tabasco. Add the shrimp, lemon juice, lemon rind and parsley. Heat through until the shrimp are cooked and flavors meld. Serve over white rice.

(Compliments of former employee Koleen Little, a native of Louisiana)

Castle Garden Gate, collection of Catherine and Robert Stallworth.
View from inside the garden at 14th century Broughton Castle
in the Cotswolds, England.

Asparagus Casserole

7 to 8 Saltine Crackers, crushed

1.25 pounds (1 small bunch) Fresh Asparagus, washed

8.5 ounces LeSueur Peas, drained

2 (2-ounce) packages Slivered Almonds

Cheese Sauce:

   ½ stick Butter

   2 Tbl. Flour

   1 cup Purity Dairy Milk

   2 (5-ounce) jars Kraft Old English Cheese

   Tabasco Sauce to taste

   ½ tsp. Salt

   ¼ tsp. Pepper

Sprinkle half of the cracker crumbs in the bottom of a small casserole dish. Snap the tough ends off the asparagus and discard. Cut the remaining stems into 3 pieces. Steam the asparagus until tender, but firm. Over the cracker crumbs, layer half of the asparagus, half the can of peas, and one package of almonds.

Cheese Sauce: Melt the butter over medium heat and add the flour to make a roux, stirring with the backside of a fork until smooth. Gradually add the milk and stir with a wire whisk until the sauce is thick and bubbly. Add the cheese and stir until melted. Add the Tabasco, salt and pepper and stir well.

Pour half of the cheese sauce over the almond layer. Repeat the layers again, ending with the crushed crackers. Bake uncovered in a 325° oven for 30 minutes or until bubbly.

(Compliments of my sister Suzan Putman and revised by my daughter Kristi Stone Elzinga)

Candied Yams

4 pounds Sweet Potatoes

3½ cups Granulated Sugar

1 cup Water

½ cup Brown Sugar

¼ tsp. Ground Nutmeg

½ fresh Lemon, with peel

½ fresh Orange, with peel

Boil the potatoes for 30 minutes or until tender. Drain and allow to cool. Peel and cut the potatoes into ½" slices and place in a greased casserole dish.

In a saucepan combine the water, sugar, brown sugar and nutmeg. Mix well and squeeze in the juices from the lemon and orange. Add the peels to the mixture and bring to a boil. Reduce the heat and simmer for 20 minutes. Remove the lemon and orange peels from the mixture.

Pour the syrup over the potatoes, cover with aluminum foil, and bake in a preheated 350° oven for 1 hour.

(Compliments of employee Fernando Rodriquez)

Corn Pudding

(Serves 8)

2 cups canned Shoepeg White Corn, drained

½ cup Purity Dairy Milk

2 Tbl. Granulated Sugar

½ tsp. Baking Powder

1 tsp. Salt

2 Eggs, beaten

1 Tbl. Cornstarch

¼ cup Butter, melted

Combine all of the ingredients and mix well. Pour the pudding into a greased 1 quart casserole dish. Bake in a preheated 350° oven for 1 hour or until a knife inserted in the center comes out clean. Be careful not to overcook.

(Compliments of my friend Mamie Mason)

Classic Squash

(Serves 6 to 8)

5 to 6 Yellow Squash, sliced

¼ cup Onion, chopped

⅓ cup Green Bell Pepper, diced

1½ cups Rice, cooked

1 Egg

10.5 ounce can Cream of Chicken Soup

¼ cup Mayonnaise

¼ cup Purity Dairy Milk

½ tsp. Salt

½ tsp. Pepper

2½ cups Cheddar Cheese, grated – *for topping*

Boil the squash in water for 10 minutes or until tender. Drain and mash with a potato masher. Again, drain any excess water. Add the remaining ingredients to the squash and stir well. Pour the mixture into a greased 10"x14" casserole dish. Sprinkle with the cheese and bake in a preheated 350° oven for 30 minutes.

(Compliments of my friend Carol Boeing)

Onion Rice

(Serves 6)

2 Tbl. Butter

7 ounce can sliced Mushrooms, drained well

½ cup Uncle Ben's Regular Rice

10.5 ounce can French Onion Soup

½ cup Water

Melt the butter in sauce pan and sauté the mushrooms. Add the rice and continue to sauté until brownish in color. Add the soup and water. Cover and simmer over low heat until the water is absorbed – approximately 20 to 25 minutes.

(Compliments of my Aunt Elva Scobey)

Potato Casserole

2 pound bag Hash-Brown Potatoes, thawed

¼ cup Onions, chopped

10.5 ounce can Cream of Chicken Soup

½ stick Butter, melted

½ pound Cheddar Cheese, grated

Potato Chips, crushed – *for topping*

Combine all of the ingredients except for the crushed chips and place in a greased 9"x11" pan. Top with the crushed chips. Bake in a preheated 350° oven for 45 minutes.

Creamy Carrot Casserole

Carrots with a zing!

1½ pounds Carrots, peeled and sliced or 20 ounce bag frozen sliced
   Carrots, thawed

1 cup Mayonnaise

1 Tbl. Onion, grated

1 Tbl. Prepared Horseradish

Toppings:

¼ cup Cheddar Cheese, shredded

½ to 1 cup Breadcrumbs

In a saucepan, cook the carrots in water just to cover until crisp-tender. Drain the water, reserving ¼ cup of the cooking liquid. Place the carrots in a greased 1½ quart baking dish.

In a separate bowl, combine the mayonnaise, onion, horseradish and carrot liquid. Pour the mixture over the carrots. Sprinkle with cheese and top with breadcrumbs. Bake in a preheated 350° oven for 30 minutes.

Eggplant Parmesan

Simply wonderful!

1 (2 pound) Eggplant
2 Eggs, slightly beaten
3 Tbl. Water
½ tsp. Salt
⅓ cup Flour
½ cup Italian Breadcrumbs
1 cup Olive Oil
32 ounce can Tomato Sauce (with oregano, garlic, salt and pepper)
¼ pound Parmesan Cheese
8 ounces Mozzarella Cheese, or more if desired

Peel the eggplant and cut into ¼" slices. Mix the eggs, water and salt. Dip the eggplant slices in the flour – then in egg mixture – and finally in the breadcrumbs to coat evenly.

In a large skillet, heat ¼ cup olive oil over medium heat. Cook the coated eggplant until lightly brown on both sides. Add the remaining olive oil as needed. Drain on paper towels.

Assembly: Pour half of the tomato sauce in the bottom of a shallow 3 quart baking dish. Layer the eggplant, parmesan cheese and mozzarella. Repeat the layering, ending with the cheese. Top with the remaining tomato sauce. Bake uncovered in a preheated 350° oven for 45 minutes.

Lynda's Homemade Dressing

(Serves 8 to 10)

Happy Holidays!

2 to 3 cups cooked Biscuits, crumbled and extra dry

6 cups cooked Cornbread, crumbled and dry

1 cup Butter

1½ cups Onions, diced

1½ cups Celery, diced

8 cups Chicken Broth

2 Eggs

Sage to taste

Salt & Pepper to taste

The day before preparing the dressing, make the biscuits and cornbread. Crumble the breads and set aside to dry.

The next day, sauté the onion and celery in the butter until just tender. In a separate bowl, blend the chicken broth and eggs. Set aside.

Add the sage, salt and pepper to the crumbled cornbread and biscuits. Combine this mixture, along with the celery mixture, to the chicken broth mixture. The dressing should be very moist with extra liquid around edges to allow the dressing to remain moist after baking.

Pour the dressing into a 9"x11" baking dish greased with shortening. Bake uncovered in a preheated 350° oven for 45 minutes. During the last 15 minutes of baking, with a fork pull the 'more done' sides to the middle of the casserole to allow for the 'less done' middle to move to the outer edges. This will ensure even cooking throughout.

Nui Nui's Macaroni & Cheese

(Serves 12)

This casserole is lighter than traditional macaroni and cheese and one of my favorites. If you prefer more liquid, use less Rigatoni.

¼ cup Butter

1 pound bag Rigatoni, cooked al dente and drained

1 pound Hoop Cheddar Cheese, thickly sliced

2 cups Half-and-Half

3 cups Purity Dairy Milk

2 Eggs, slightly beaten

Tabasco Sauce to taste

Salt & Pepper to taste

Place the butter in a 9"x11" Pyrex dish and allow it to melt in a preheated 350° oven. Layer the Rigatoni over the butter and liberally add the cheese. Place the cheese at angles to allow it to reach the bottom of the pan at random.

In a separate bowl combine the Half-and-Half, milk, eggs, Tabasco, salt and pepper. Pour this mixture over the casserole. Bake in the preheated 350° oven for 45 minutes or until the liquid sets.

Vegetable Casserole

You may think that nothing wonderful can come from a can of "Veg-All," but just try this recipe – what a surprise!

2 (16-ounce) cans Veg-All, drained
½ cup Onion, chopped
¾ stick Margarine, melted
¾ cup Sour Cream
1 cup Celery, chopped
¾ cup Mayonnaise
1 cup Cheddar Cheese, grated

Toppings:
Parmesan Cheese
½ cup Ritz Crackers, crushed

Combine the Veg-All with the remaining main ingredients and mix well by hand. Pour into a baking dish and sprinkle with the parmesan cheese and crackers. Bake in a preheated 325° oven for 30 minutes.

Spinach Casserole

This spicy dish is a wonderful accompaniment to turkey and sweet potatoes – a great holiday dish!

2 (10-ounce) packages Frozen Chopped Spinach

4 Tbl. Butter

2 Tbl. Onion, chopped (more if desired)

2 heaping Tbl. Flour

½ cup Spinach Liquid

½ cup Evaporated Milk

6 ounce roll Jalapeño Cheese

½ tsp. Pepper

½ tsp. fresh Garlic, chopped

1 tsp. Worcestershire Sauce

6 ounce can Water Chestnuts, sliced

Breadcrumbs – *for topping*

Cook the spinach according to the package directions and drain, reserving the liquid. Set both aside.

Melt the butter and sauté the onion. Slowly add the flour to the butter and onions, constantly stirring with a wire whisk or fork to make a roux. Slowly add the spinach liquid and the milk. Allow the mixture to thicken, whisking until smooth. Add the jalapeño cheese and stir to create a thick sauce. Season with pepper, garlic and Worcestershire.

Add the drained spinach and water chestnuts. Stir the mixture well and pour into a greased casserole dish. Lightly sprinkle breadcrumbs over the top. Bake in a preheated 350° oven for 30 to 45 minutes or until bubbly.

Spinach Cheese Pie

Crust:

- 8 ounces Cream Cheese, softened
- 1 cup Butter
- 2 cups Flour, sifted

Filling:

- 1 large Onion, chopped
- 3 Tbl. Vegetable Oil
- 2 (6-ounce) rolls Jalapeño Cheese
- ½ tsp. Salt
- 2 (10-ounce) packages Frozen Spinach, thawed and squeezed dry
- 1 Egg

Crust: Mix the cream cheese and the butter and cut into the flour until the dough gathers together. Press the mixture into two balls. Cover and chill until the dough is firm. Roll out both dough balls into pie shell shapes and place one of the shells in a pie plate. Reserve the other pie shell for the top.

Filling: Sauté the onion in the oil. Drain the oil. Over very low heat, add the jalapeño cheese to the onion, stirring until the cheese melts. Remove the mixture from the heat and add the remaining ingredients, stirring well. Pour the mixture into the pie crust.

Lay the reserved pie crust on top of the mixture, pinching the dough together to secure the edges. Prick the top of the crust with a fork to allow steam to escape. Bake in a preheated 325° oven for 70 minutes.

Sweet Potato Casserole

4 cups canned or freshly baked Sweet Potatoes,
  cooked and mashed if fresh – drained and mashed if canned

½ cup Butter, softened

½ cup Brown Sugar

⅔ cup Heavy Cream

1 Egg, slightly beaten

Salt to taste

2 tsp. Vanilla

Streusel Topping:

  1 cup Brown Sugar

  ½ cup Flour

  ½ cup Pecans

  ¼ cup Butter, cut in small pieces

With a mixer, beat the sweet potatoes until the lumps are nearly gone. Slowly beat in the butter and brown sugar. In a separate bowl, mix the heavy cream and egg and add to the sweet potato mixture. Mix well. Adjust the flavor with salt and vanilla. Pour into a baking dish.

Topping: Combine the brown sugar, flour, and pecans and gently add the butter with a fork. The mixture should be crumbly. Sprinkle over the casserole.

Bake uncovered in a preheated 350° oven for 45 minutes.

Sweet Potato Pudding

Although this recipe takes some preparation, it is well worth the effort. It should be served hot from the oven.

4 cups Sweet Potatoes, uncooked and grated

1 to 1½ cups Granulated Sugar

1 cup Purity Dairy Milk

4 Eggs, slightly beaten

1½ tsp. Vanilla

½ stick Butter, melted

2 tsp. Nutmeg

Combine all of the ingredients and mix well. Pour into a greased baking dish and bake in a preheated 350° oven for 45 minutes. During baking, gently stir the casserole away from the sides to allow for even cooking. Serve immediately.

Zucchini Squash Bake

2 Eggs, separated
1 cup Sour Cream
2 Tbl. Flour
6 cups thinly sliced Squash, steamed and drained
1½ cups Cheddar Cheese, shredded
¼ cup real Bacon, cooked and crumbled

Toppings:
1 Tbl. Butter, melted
¼ cup Breadcrumbs

Mix the egg yolks, sour cream and flour. Separately, beat the egg whites until stiff and then fold into the flour mixture.

Layer half of the squash, half of the egg mixture and half of the cheese in a 9" square glass dish. Sprinkle with half of the bacon crumbles. Repeat the layering.

Mix the butter and breadcrumbs and sprinkle over the top of the casserole. Bake in a preheated 350° oven for 30 minutes or until bubbly.

This dish can be served without the topping if preferred.

(Compliments of employee Beverly Puckett)

White Roses, Red Roses, collection of Andrea and Wayne Richard.
Some roses I viewed while on a Rose Society tour in Nashville, Tennessee.

Brown Sugar Cookies

This is the cookie recipe that I remember from my childhood. It's the kind of cookie my mother kept in one of those old-fashioned cookie tins and we enjoyed for several weeks during the holiday season. She usually topped them with multi-colored non-pareils before baking. The longer they stayed in the tin, the better they were! The dough works very well in a cookie press.

1 pound Butter, room temperature

1 cup Brown Sugar

2 tsp. Vanilla

4 to 5 cups Flour

With a mixer on low, cream together the butter and brown sugar until fluffy and light in color. Add the vanilla and flour 1 cup at a time and mix until the dough is no longer sticky to the fingers. Roll the dough into small balls and place on a cookie sheet. Flatten with the bottom of a glass and sprinkle with non-pareils or colored sugar. Bake in a preheated 350° oven for 15 minutes.

(Compliments of my mother Alyce Scobey)

O'Henry Bars

⅔ cup Butter

4 cups Oatmeal, uncooked

1 cup Brown Sugar

½ cup Light Corn Syrup

3 tsp. Vanilla

6 ounces Chocolate Chips

⅔ cups Peanut Butter

Cream the butter with a mixer and stir in the oatmeal, brown sugar, corn syrup and vanilla. Spread the mixture in a 9"x13" pan. Bake in a preheated 350° oven for 15 minutes. Remove from the oven and allow this layer to cool.

In a sauce pan or microwave, melt the chocolate chips and peanut butter together. Spread this mixture over the cooled layer. Refrigerate for several hours before cutting into squares.

(Compliments of Marcy Batterton, Front-End Manager)

Brownies

8 ounces Unsweetened Chocolate

1 pound Butter, melted

4 cups Granulated Sugar

2 cups Flour

¼ cup Vanilla

8 Eggs

Melt the chocolate and butter in the microwave. With a wire whisk, add the sugar mixed with the flour. Lastly, add the vanilla and eggs and beat with wire whisk for two minutes. Pour the mixture into a greased deep-sided cookie sheet. Bake in a preheated 350° oven for 45 minutes.

Brownies with Chocolate Icing

(Yields Several Large Pans)

1 pound Butter

12 ounces Bitter Chocolate Squares

2 cups Flour

4 cups Granulated Sugar

8 Eggs

¼ cup Vanilla Flavoring

Chocolate Icing:

16 ounces Bitter Chocolate

2 sticks Margarine

1¼ cups Water

Powdered Sugar

Combine and melt the butter and chocolate in the microwave. In a separate bowl, combine the flour and sugar until thoroughly mixed. With a wire whisk, add the flour mixture to the chocolate mixture. Stir in the eggs and vanilla until the mixture turns glossy and becomes thick. Before the mixture looses its sheen or becomes too thick, pour it into greased and floured pans.

Bake in a preheated 350° oven for 30 to 40 minutes. The brownies will just begin to pull away from the sides of pan when they are done. Be sure not to overcook – brownies must be moist.

Chocolate Icing: Combine and melt the chocolate, margarine and water in the microwave. With a wire whisk or a mixer, add the powdered sugar a bit at a time to reach the desired thickness. Using a cake spatula, ice the cooled brownies.

Butter Crunch

1 stick Butter

1 stick Margarine

1 cup Granulated Sugar

2 Hershey's Milk Chocolate Bars

1 cup Pecans, finely chopped

In a heavy sauce pan cook the butter, margarine and sugar over medium heat — stirring constantly. When the mixture turns caramel in color, remove it from the heat and pour onto an ungreased cookie sheet with sides.

Break the chocolate bars into bite-size pieces and sprinkle over the hot mixture. When the chocolate has melted, swirl a knife over the top. Sprinkle with pecans. This candy can be placed in the refrigerator to cool before breaking into pieces with a knife or ice pick.

Cherry Jewels

4 sticks Butter

1 cup Granulated Sugar

4 Egg Yolks

4 tsp. Grated Lemon Rind

4 tsp. Vanilla

4 tsp. Lemon Juice

4 tsp. Orange Juice

5 cups Flour, sifted

Pecans, finely chopped

Candied Cherry Halves (½ cherry per cookie)

With a mixer, cream the butter and sugar until the mixture is fluffy. Add the egg yolks, lemon rind, vanilla and juices. Gradually beat in the flour. Allow the dough to chill for 2 hours.

Form the dough into 1" balls and roll them in the pecans. Place on a greased cookie sheet and press a cherry half on each cookie. Bake in a preheated 350° oven for 10 to 12 minutes.

(Compliments of my mother Alyce Scobey)

Chocolate Revel Bars

1 cup Butter

2 cups Brown Sugar

2 Eggs

2 tsp. Vanilla

2½ cups Flour

1 tsp. Baking Soda

1 tsp. Salt

3 cups Oatmeal

Filling:

12 ounces Chocolate Chips

15 ounces Sweetened Condensed Milk

2 Tbl. Butter

½ tsp. Salt

1 cup Pecan pieces

2 tsp. Vanilla

With a mixer, cream the butter and sugar until light. Add the eggs and vanilla. Fluff the flour with a spoon and add the flour, baking soda and salt to the butter mixture. Mix well and add the oatmeal.

Filling: In a saucepan over low heat, melt the chocolate chips, condensed milk, butter and salt together. Stir often so it doesn't burn. When the mixture is smooth, add the nuts and vanilla.

Spread two-thirds of the oatmeal mixture in a greased 15½"x10½"x1" baking pan. Cover this layer with the filling and top with the remaining oatmeal mixture. Bake in preheated 350° oven for 25 to 30 minutes.

(Compliments of former employee Bonnie Yockman)

Crispy Caramel Corn

2 cups Brown Sugar

1 cup Margarine

½ cup White Corn Syrup

1 tsp. Salt

1 tsp. Vanilla

½ tsp. Baking Soda

7 quarts Popped Corn mixed with 1 cup Peanuts

In a heavy sauce pan (allowing for an extra 4" at the top for foam to rise), combine the sugar, margarine, corn syrup and salt. Bring the mixture to a boil and boil for 5 minutes. Remove from the heat and stir in the vanilla and baking soda. Foam will instantly form when the baking soda is added. Immediately pour the mixture over freshly popped corn and peanuts in a large container. Mix well and quickly. Pour onto two cookie sheets lined with foil.

Bake in a preheated 200° oven for 1 hour 45 minutes, stirring every 15 minutes. Store in a tightly sealed container as air will make the corn soggy.

Easter Story Cookies

This cookie will make wonderful memories for you and your children or grand-children. Make these cookies the night before Easter.

- **1 cup Whole Pecans**
- **1 tsp. Vinegar**
- **3 Egg Whites**
- **pinch of Salt**
- **1 cup Granulated Sugar**
- **1 cup Chocolate Chips**
- **Zip Lock Bag, Wooden Spoon, Tape, Bible**

Place the pecans in a zip lock bag and let the children beat and break them with a wooden spoon until the nuts are in small pieces. Explain that after Jesus was arrested, He was beaten by the Roman soldiers. (Read **John 19:1-3**)

Let the child smell the vinegar and pour it in a mixing bowl. Explain that when Jesus was thirsty on the cross He was given vinegar to drink. (Read **John 19:28-30**)

Add the egg whites to the vinegar. The eggs represent life. Explain that Jesus gave His life to give us life. (Read **John 10:10-11**) Sprinkle a pinch of salt into the child's hand and let them taste it. Brush the rest into the bowl with the egg mixture. Explain that this represents the salty tears shed by Jesus' followers and the bitterness of our sins. (Read **Luke 23:27**)

Next, add the sugar and explain that the sweetest part of this story is that Jesus died because He loves us. He wants us to know and belong to Him. (Read **Psalm 34:8** and **John 3:16**)

(continued)

Stir in the chocolate chips and beat the mixture on high for 12 to 15 minutes until stiff peaks form. Explain that the color white represents the purity in God's eyes of those whose sins have been cleansed by Jesus. (Read **Isaiah 1:18** and **John 3:1-3**)

Fold in the broken nuts. With a teaspoon drop the dough onto wax paper covering a cookie sheet. Explain that each mound represents the rocky tomb where Jesus' body was laid. (Read **Matthew 27:57-60**)

Place the cookie sheet in a preheated 300° oven. Close the door and turn the oven off. Give the child a piece of tape and seal the oven door. Explain that Jesus' tomb was sealed. (Read **Matthew 27: 65-66**)

As you and the children prepare for bed, explain that there may be sadness about leaving the cookies in the oven overnight; likewise, Jesus' followers were sad and in despair when his tomb was sealed. (Read **John 16:20-22**)

On Easter morning, open the oven and pass out the cookies. Notice the cracked surface of the cookie and take a bite. The cookies are hollow! On the first Easter Jesus' followers were amazed to find the tomb open and empty. (Read **Matthew 28:1-9**)

Delicate Sugar Cookies

1 cup Margarine

1 cup Vegetable Oil

1 cup Granulated Sugar

2 Eggs

1 tsp. Vanilla

1 tsp. Cream of Tartar

1 tsp. Baking Soda

1 tsp. Salt

4 cups Flour

1 cup Granulated Sugar – *for topping*

Cream together the margarine, oil and sugar. Add the eggs and vanilla. Sift together the remaining dry ingredients and add to the creamed mixture. Chill the dough for 4 hours and then place it in a cookie press or form into small balls and flatten with the bottom of a glass. Sprinkle the tops with sugar. Bake in a preheated 350° oven for 12 minutes.

Sugar Cookies with Glaze

1 tsp. Baking Powder

1 tsp. Vanilla

1 Egg

⅔ cup Butter, cut in 1" chunks

2 cups Flour

Glaze:

   1 cup Powdered Sugar, sifted

   1 Tbl. Water

With a mixer and paddle attachment, combine the baking powder, vanilla and egg. Add the butter and slowly add the flour. Mix well until the dough forms. Place the dough in plastic wrap and chill for 3 hours.

Roll the dough onto a floured surface to $\frac{1}{8}$" thickness. Cut into the desired shape and place on a greased cookie sheet. Bake in a preheated 375° oven for 7 minutes or until the cookie edges are lightly browned.

Glaze: Mix the powdered sugar and water. Depending on the desired consistency, increase or decrease the water. Dip the cooled cookies into the glaze and allow them to dry on a cooling rack.

(Compliments of my daughter Ali Burns,
French Pastry School – Chicago)

Heath Bar Squares

Butter

Saltine Crackers, finely crumbled

1 cup Butter

1 cup Brown Sugar

12 ounces Chocolate Chips

1½ to 2 cups Pecans or Almonds, crushed *(optional)*

Cover a large, deep cookie sheet with heavy aluminum foil and grease well with butter. Coat the entire bottom of the cookie sheet with the cracker crumbs. Heat the butter and brown sugar and boil for 3 minutes, constantly stirring. Pour the mixture over the cracker crumbs. Bake in a preheated 375° oven for 5 minutes.

Remove from the oven and sprinkle with the chocolate chips. As the chips begin to melt, spread the chocolate with a spatula. Sprinkle crushed nuts on top if desired. Refrigerate for 1 hour to set the chocolate. Cut into squares. Yummy!

(Compliments of my sister-in-law Jean Stone)

Honey Crunchies
(Yields 50)

3 cups Quick Cooking Oats

1 cup flaked Coconut

1 cup Pecans, chopped

1 cup Flour

1½ cups Brown Sugar, firmly packed

1 cup Butter

⅓ cup Honey

In a large bowl, mix the oats, coconut, pecans and flour. In a heavy sauce pan, heat the brown sugar, butter and honey until it reaches a boil. Pour the honey mixture over the dry ingredients and mix well.

Drop the dough by rounded teaspoon into greased muffin tins so that the cookies retain their shape. Bake in a preheated 350° oven for 12 to 15 minutes or until lightly browned. Cool in the pan.

(Compliments of my sister-in-law Jean Stone)

Macaroon Coconut Cookies

1 pound Granulated Sugar

8 ounces Unsweetened Coconut, grated

1 cup Egg Whites

Combine all of the ingredients in a bowl and place the bowl on top of a pot of boiling water for 1 hour. Stir occasionally. Remove the bowl and drop the mixture by rounded teaspoon onto a cookie sheet lined with wax paper. Bake in a preheated 300° oven until golden brown. Allow to cool and serve.

(Compliments of Werner Bacher,
Master Pastry Chef – Austria)

Molasses Cookies

1½ stick Margarine, melted

½ cup Molasses

1 cup Granulated Sugar

1 Egg

2¼ cups Flour

2 tsp. Baking Soda

1 tsp. Cinnamon

1 tsp. Ginger

½ tsp. Cloves

½ tsp. Salt

Cream together the margarine, molasses, sugar and egg. Add the remaining ingredients and mix well. Chill the dough overnight. Shape into small balls and roll in sugar. Do not flatten the cookies, as they will shape as they bake. Bake in a preheated 350° for 8 to 10 minutes.

Nui Nui's Crescents

1 stick Butter, softened

2 Tbl. Granulated Sugar

¼ tsp. Salt

1 tsp. Vanilla

1 cup Pecans, chopped

1¼ cup Flour, sifted

1 box Powdered Sugar

Combine all of the ingredients except for the powdered sugar and mix well. Roll the dough into 1½" balls. Bake in a preheated 300° oven for 30 minutes or until barely brown. Allow the crescents to cool and then roll each in powdered sugar.

Peanut Blossoms

1¾ cup Flour

1 tsp. Baking Soda

½ tsp. Salt

½ cup Granulated Sugar

½ cup Brown Sugar

½ cup Margarine

½ cup Crunchy Peanut Butter

1 Egg

2 Tbl. Purity Dairy Milk

1 tsp. Vanilla

48 Hershey's Chocolate Kisses

Combine all of the ingredients, except for the Chocolate Kisses, and mix well. Roll the dough into small balls and press a Chocolate Kiss in the center of each cookie. Place on an ungreased cookie sheet and bake in a preheated 375° oven for 10 minutes.

(Compliments of my mother Alyce Scobey)

Peanut Brittle

1 ½ cup Granulated Sugar

½ cup Light Karo Syrup

½ cup Hot Water

2 cups Raw Peanuts

1 Tbl. Butter

1 rounded tsp. Baking Soda

Line a baking sheet with greased aluminum foil. Boil the sugar, syrup and water until long threads form, mixing with a wooden spoon. Test for 'threads' by lifting the spoon out of the syrup and let the hot liquid fall back into the pan. When long threads form, the syrup is ready. Add the peanuts and cook until the mixture begins to brown. When golden brown, add the butter and remove from the heat.

Stir in the baking soda – the mixture will immediately foam. Ensure that your sauce pan is large enough to allow for the expanding foam. Stir slightly and pour the mixture onto the baking sheet. After it has cooled on top, turn the entire slab of Peanut Brittle over to allow to cool. Break the cooled candy into pieces.

Lemon Sauce

This sauce is delightful on gingerbread, pound cake, and angel food cake.

¾ cups Granulated Sugar

2 Tbl. Flour

juice of 1 Orange

juice of 2 Lemons

2 Eggs, beaten

½ pint Whipping Cream

In a sauce pan, combine the sugar and flour. Add the orange and lemon juices and eggs. Cook until thick. Allow the sauce to cool. In a separate bowl, whip the whipping cream and add it to the lemon sauce, mixing well.

(Compliments of my Aunt Elva Scobey, from her friend Cathy)

Hot Fudge Sauce

(Yields 1½ cups)

¼ cup Cocoa

pinch of Salt

¾ cup Granulated Sugar

¼ cup Butter

1 ounce Unsweetened Chocolate

½ cup Evaporated Milk

½ tsp. Vanilla

Blend the cocoa, salt and sugar in a small bowl.

In a saucepan over low heat, melt the butter and chocolate. Slowly stir in the cocoa mixture to form a grainy paste. Gradually add the evaporated milk and stir continually until the sauce is thick and shiny and the sugar is dissolved. Remove the saucepan from the heat and stir in the vanilla.

Serve over ice cream, pound cake or just about anything that needs a dose of chocolate. *Or try this:* Cut un-iced brownies into squares and top with ice cream and hot fudge sauce.

(Compliments of employee Sherri Farr)

Mint Chocolate Ice Cream Dessert

one half gallon Breyers Chocolate Mint Ice Cream

18 Oreo Cookies, crushed in blender

½ cup Chocolate Syrup

red or green Food Coloring *(optional)*

Chocolate Curls – *for garnish*

Allow the ice cream to soften in a large mixing bowl while preparing the recipe. The ice cream will be ready when it is slightly soft and you can just begin to stir it with a spoon. It should not be runny. If you desire pink or mint green ice cream, add 2 to 3 drops of the appropriate food coloring into the softened ice cream and stir well.

Place the Oreo crumbs in an 11"x14" casserole dish. Gently drizzle chocolate syrup over the crumbs. Carefully cover the crumbs with the softened ice cream. Cover with foil and freeze until ready to serve. Cut the dessert into squares and garnish with chocolate curls (see page 141).

(Compliments of my friend Carol Boeing)

Vanilla Ice Cream

This is a 50-year-old recipe from my grandmother, Mildred Scobey, and has become a 4th of July tradition in our home. What a special treat to have homemade ice cream on a hot, summer day!

4 to 5 Eggs

1 quart Purity Dairy Milk

1 to 2 cups Granulated Sugar

½ pt. Whipping Cream

1 quart Half-and-Half

Beat the eggs and add the milk slowly. Gradually, add the sugar and cook the mixture over a double boiler until it is thick enough to coat a wooden spoon, stirring often. Allow the mixture to cool. Add the whipping cream and Half-and-Half. Place in an ice cream freezer and freeze until set.

Option: Fruit and other topping may be added halfway through the freezing process.

Sliced Peaches

Sliced Strawberries

Blueberries

Chocolate Shavings

Crushed Candy Canes (good way to use Christmas candy)

Crushed Heath Bars

Baked Chocolate Pudding

8 ounces Semi-Sweet Chocolate, broken

2 cups Heavy Whipping Cream, scalded

¼ cup Granulated Sugar

4 Eggs

⅛ tsp. Salt

1 tsp. Vanilla

Place the chocolate pieces in a blender and pour in the hot, scalded cream. Mix well. With the blender on, add the sugar and eggs one at a time through the top feed hole. Blend until smooth and shiny. Add the salt and vanilla. Pour the mixture into a buttered 1 quart baking dish and bake in a preheated 325° oven for 60 to 70 minutes. Serve with a dollop of cream or sweetened whipped cream.

(Compliments of employee Sherri Farr)

Crème Brulee

1 cup Half-and-Half
½ Vanilla Bean, split and pulp scraped
¼ cup Granulated Sugar
3 Egg Yolks
2 tsp. Granulated Sugar

In a sauce pan combine the Half-and-Half and vanilla bean with the pulp. Bring the mixture to a simmer. *Suggestion:* At this point, you can flavor the custard with your favorite liqueur or steep your favorite tea, such as Earl Grey or Chamomile, in cream mixture.

In a mixing bowl, whisk the sugar into the egg yolks until the mixture is very fluffy. Combine the cream mixture with the egg mixture and allow to cool slightly. Pour the mixture into two 6 ounce ramekins. Bake in a water bath in a preheated 350° oven for 30 to 40 minutes or until the custard is set.

When ready to serve, sprinkle the sugar evenly over the tops of the custard and caramelize the sugar with a propane torch or under the oven broiler.

(Compliments of Alexandra Mattea, Pastry Chef,
Dubrulle French Culinary School – Vancouver British Columbia)

Banana Pudding

(Serves 10 when doubled)

This recipe is not as easy as the Jell-O pudding type, but it is well worth the effort. Trust me – you'll want to double the recipe because it will only last for a few days in the refrigerator if your family doesn't eat it first.

⅔ cup Granulated Sugar

¼ tsp. Salt

5 Tbl. Flour

2 cups Purity Dairy Milk

3 Eggs

2 Tbl. Butter

1 tsp. Vanilla

¾ of a 12 ounce box Nabisco Nilla Vanilla Wafers

4 to 5 Bananas, sliced coin-size

Combine the sugar, salt and flour. Slowly add the milk and cook over a double boiler until the mixture is thick, and then cook for an additional 2 minutes. Add the eggs and cook for 1 minute. Remove from the heat and add the butter and vanilla.

Layer half of the wafers and half of the bananas in a 7"x11" glass baking dish (if doubled). Top the wafers with half of the pudding. Repeat the layers of wafers, bananas and pudding. You may want to top with whipping cream.

(Compliments of my friend Phyllis Northcutt)

Chocolate Layer Dessert

Crust:
- 1 cup Flour
- 2 Tbl. Granulated Sugar
- ½ cup Pecans, chopped
- 1 stick Margarine, melted

First Layer:
- 8 ounces Cream Cheese
- 1 cup Granulated Sugar
- 8 ounces Cool Whip

Second Layer:
- 3.5 ounces Chocolate Pudding, cook and serve – not instant
- 3.5 ounces Vanilla Pudding, cook and serve – not instant
- 3 cups Purity Dairy Milk

Toppings:
- 8 ounces Cool Whip
- Chocolate Curls (page 141)

Crust: Combine all of the crust ingredients and mix well. Press into a 9"x11" pan. Bake in a preheated 350° oven for 15 to 18 minutes. Allow to cool completely.

First Layer: Combine all of the ingredients for the first layer and mix well. Spread over the cooled crust and place in the refrigerator.

Second Layer: In a saucepan, combine all of the ingredients for the second layer and cook over low heat until the pudding bubbles and thickens. Allow the mixture to cool completely and spread it over the first layer.

Top the dessert with the remaining Cool Whip and chocolate curls.

(Compliments of my mother Alyce Scobey)

Chocolate Curls

Chocolate curls are a wonderful garnish for many desserts. Delicate chocolate curls take a dessert from great to extraordinary. The technique takes time to accomplish, but the results will be well worth the effort. The thicker the bar or block of chocolate, the larger the curls will be. You may use semisweet or bittersweet chocolate squares, or in a pinch, a solid chocolate bar will work. Don't forget about white chocolate, too. However, white chocolate is harder to work with because it is softer. Take care not to touch the curls because they melt easily.

Place the chocolate block on a plate in a warm spot (by a sunny window, on the stovetop, or even under a hot lamp) for 1 hour just to lightly soften. Drag a sharp vegetable peeler down one side of the chocolate in one motion from top to bottom to create curls, which will vary in size. Leftover curls can be stored in a zipper bag in the freezer for up to 1 month. If you are using the curls the same day, transfer them to a sheet of aluminum foil and refrigerate.

Basic Buttercream Frosting

1 pound Butter, room temperature

1 pound Crisco

1 tsp. Almond or Clear Vanilla Extract

2 pounds Powdered Sugar, sifted

Combine the butter and Crisco in a mixer, beating on low until smooth. Continually scrape the sides of the mixer. Add your choice of flavoring and gradually add the powdered sugar.

To make chocolate buttercream, omit the extract and instead add ½ cup unsweetened cocoa.

(Compliments of my daughter Ali Burns,
French Pastry School – Chicago)

Coffee Ice Cream Dessert with Butterscotch Sauce

(Serves 8 to10)

22 Oreo Cookies, finely crumbled

3 Tbl. Butter, softened

1 gallon Coffee Ice Cream, slightly softened

Butterscotch Sauce:

1 cup Brown Sugar

½ cup Granulated Sugar

⅔ cup Evaporated Milk

¼ cup Butter

¼ tsp. Salt

1 tsp. Vanilla

Combine the cookies and butter and press into a 10" pie pan. Bake in a preheated 300° oven for $2\frac{1}{2}$ minutes or until heated through. Allow the crust to cool and top with the ice cream. Freeze until ready to serve.

Butterscotch Sauce: Mix both sugars, the milk, butter and salt and cook over low heat for 3 minutes. Remove from the heat and stir in the vanilla. Pour the sauce over the dessert before serving.

Bavarian Apple Torte

Crust:

½ cup Butter

⅓ cup Granulated Sugar

½ tsp. Vanilla

1 cup flour

Filling:

16 ounces Cream Cheese, softened

½ cup Granulated Sugar

2 Eggs

1 tsp. Vanilla

Topping:

4 cups firm, tart Apples, peeled, cored and thinly sliced

⅓ cup Granulated Sugar

½ tsp. Cinnamon

Crust: With a mixer, cream the butter and sugar. Gradually add the vanilla and flour and mix well. Spread the dough into the bottom of a greased 9" springform pan.

Filling: With a mixer, blend the cream cheese and sugar. Add the eggs and vanilla and beat well. Pour the filling into the uncooked crust.

Topping: In a large bowl, thoroughly coat the apples with the sugar and cinnamon. Decoratively place the coated apples on the top of the filling – be creative.

Bake in a preheated 450° oven for 5 minutes. Turn the oven down to 400° and bake an additional 25 minutes. Allow the pie to cool and take in the delightful aroma. Enjoy!

(Compliments of my daughter Ali Burns,
French Pastry School – Chicago)

Frozen Raspberry Delight

This is my granddaughter Rachel's favorite dessert.

Crust:

> 2 cups crushed Oreos, centers removed
>
> ⅓ cup Margarine or Butter, melted
>
> ¼ cup Granulated Sugar

Filling:

> 1 cup Chocolate Fudge Sauce
>
> 1 quart Vanilla Ice Cream, slightly softened
>
> 1 pint Raspberry Sherbet, slightly softened

Topping:

> 8 ounces frozen Cool Whip, thawed
>
> 12 ounce package Frozen Raspberries, without syrup
>
> ¼ cup of Crust

Crust: Combine all of the crust ingredients and mix well. Reserve ¼ cup for the topping. Press the remaining crust in a 13"x9" pan. Refrigerate for 15 minutes.

Filling: Spread the fudge sauce over the cooled crust and top with ice cream. Randomly place spoonfuls of sherbet over the ice cream layer. Gently swirl the sherbet into the ice cream.

Topping: Spread the Cool Whip over the sherbet/ice cream layer and gently swirl. Top with raspberries, pressing them firmly into ice cream/ sherbet mixture. Sprinkle the top with the reserved crust crumbs.

Cover and freeze for 6 hours or overnight. Allow the dessert to stand at room temperature for 10 to 15 minutes before serving.

(Compliments of my Aunt Elva Scobey)

Limeade Dessert

If you are serving this to guests, double the recipe. It will be a hit!

Crust:

1 cup Flour
½ cup Light Brown Sugar
½ cup Almonds, chopped
1 stick Butter

Ginger Ice Cream:

2 to 3 cups Vanilla Ice Cream
¼ cup Crystallized Ginger, finely chopped
½ cup Frozen Limeade, undiluted

Crust: Combine the crust ingredients and mix well. Place in a 9" square pan and bake in a preheated 325° for 15 to 20 minutes. Stir several times during baking to crumble. Reserve some of the cooked crust for the topping.

Ginger Ice Cream: Combine the ingredients and pour over the cooled, crumbled crust. Freeze overnight.

Before serving, sprinkle the top with the reserved bits of crust.

(Compliments of my Aunt Mil)

French Ganache

This icing is great to pour over a Bundt Cake or any dessert that deserves a dose of chocolate over the top. If you need to make more than 2 cups, simply add equal parts of the ingredients.

1 cup Semi Sweet Chocolate Chips (imported if available)

1 cup Heavy Cream

Place the chocolate in a large bowl. Pour the cream in a saucepan and heat until it just comes to a boil. Pour the cream over the chocolate and allow it to sit a few minutes, stirring occasionally with a wire whisk. Ganache stays soft to touch and should be refrigerated.

Peppermint Party Dessert

This dessert is a lovely presentation for a summer bridal shower or tea. Yummy!

4 (1-ounce) squares Semi-Sweet Chocolate, melted

8 ounce can Chocolate Syrup

3 to 4 cups Rice Krispies

½ gallon or more Peppermint Ice Cream

Toppings:

12 ounce jar Pineapple Preserves

½ cup Crème de Menthe

In a saucepan over low heat, combine the semi-sweet chocolate and chocolate syrup until the chocolate is completely melted. Add the Rice Krispies, mix well, and pat the crust into a 9"x11" buttered pan. Top with the ice cream and place in the freezer overnight.

Topping: Before serving, cut into squares. Place on plates and spoon on toppings.

Strawberry Dumplings

1 pound Cream Cheese

2 ounces Flour

2 ounces Cornmeal

2 ounces Granulated Sugar

1 Egg

Topping:

2 Tbl. Butter

1 cup Sweet Breadcrumbs or Cookie Crumbs

1 Tbl. Granulated Sugar

8 medium Strawberries

Powdered Sugar – *for dusting*

Combine all of the main ingredients and mix well. Allow the mixture to sit in a cool place for 30 minutes.

Topping: In a small saucepan, heat the butter until it is melted and lightly brown. Mix in the sweet cookie crumbs and sugar.

Cover the strawberries with half of the cream cheese mixture and form the dumplings. Drop the dumplings one at a time into a large pot of boiling water. When the dumplings bounce back to the water's surface, remove them and place on a dish and dust with extra cookie crumbs and powdered sugar. Serve hot.

(Compliments of Werner Bacher,
Master Pastry Chef – Austria)

Banana Hazelnut Coffeecake

6 ounces Butter

2 Tbl. + 1 tsp. Vanilla

1½ cup Bananas, pureed

3 Eggs

1½ cups Granulated Sugar

3 cups Cake Flour

1½ tsp. Baking Powder

½ tsp. Baking Soda

1½ tsp. Salt

Toppings:

1½ cups Granulated Sugar

3 cups Hazelnuts, toasted

In a small saucepan over low heat, melt the butter and add the vanilla and bananas. Set aside.

Whisk the eggs and gradually add the sugar. Mix until light and fluffy. Gently fold into the banana mixture.

In a bowl, combine the flour, baking powder, baking soda and salt and whisk until well incorporated. Fold the dry ingredients into the banana mixture. Pour into two 9" greased and floured round cake pans.

In a food processor, blend the sugar and hazelnuts and sprinkle on top of the batter. Bake in a preheated 350° oven for 40 minutes or until a toothpick comes out clean from the center of the cake.

(Compliments of Pastry Chef Sam Tucker)

Chocolate Cookie Sheet Cake

This is so simple to make, but oh, so delicious! If unexpected guests arrive, this cake is easy to make in very little time and you probably will have all of the ingredients on hand.

2 sticks Butter

4 Tbl. Cocoa

1 cup Water

2 cups Flour

2 cups Granulated Sugar

1 tsp. Baking Soda

1 tsp. Vanilla

½ cup Purity Dairy Buttermilk

2 Eggs

Icing:

6 Tbl. Purity Dairy Milk

4 Tbl. Cocoa

1 stick Butter, softened

1 Tbl. Vanilla

1 box Powdered Sugar

Mix the butter, cocoa and water in a sauce pan and bring to a boil. In a separate bowl, combine the flour and sugar. Pour the cocoa mixture over the flour. Add the baking soda, vanilla, buttermilk and eggs and mix well. Pour the batter onto a greased cookie sheet pan with sides. Bake in a preheated 350° oven for 30 minutes.

Icing: Bring the milk, cocoa and butter to a boil. Add the vanilla and powdered sugar. Mix well with a wire whisk and pour over the cake while still hot.

(Compliments of my mother Alyce Scobey)

Chocolate Zucchini Cake

4 Eggs

½ cup Corn Oil

3 cups Granulated Sugar

3 cups Zucchini, grated

3 cups Flour

1 ½ tsp. Baking Powder

1 tsp. Baking Soda

1 tsp. Salt

1 ½ tsp. Cinnamon

2 squares Unsweetened Chocolate, melted

1 cup chopped nuts *(optional)*

Frosting:

3 ounces Cream Cheese

1 Tbl. Butter

2 cups Confectioners Sugar

With a mixer, beat the eggs. Add the oil, sugar and zucchini. Mix until well blended.

In a separate bowl, sift together the dry ingredients and add to the egg mixture, blending well. Add the chocolate and fold in the nuts. Pour the batter into a well greased 10 cup tube pan and bake in a preheated 350° oven for 1 hour 30 minutes – or in a 9"x13"x2" pan for 1 hour. Allow to cool.

Frosting: Combine all of the frosting ingredients and mix well. Ice the cake or simply dust the top with powdered sugar.

(Compliments of employee Beverly Puckett)

Chocolate Walnut Cheesecake

Crust:

 1 cup Chocolate Wafer Crumbs

 ½ cup Walnuts, finely chopped

 4 Tbl. Butter, melted

 2 Tbl. Granulated Sugar

 2 Tbl. Bitter Chocolate, melted

Filling:

 24 ounces Cream Cheese

 4 Eggs

 1 cup Granulated Sugar

 6 ounces Semi-Sweet Chocolate Chips

 10 to 11 Tbl. Butter

 1 cup Sour Cream

 1 ½ tsp. Vanilla

 pinch of Salt

 ¾ cup Walnuts, chopped

Garnish:

 Sweetened Whipped Cream

Crust: Combine all of the crust ingredients and mix well. Press into a buttered 8" springform pan. Chill.

Filling: Using an electric mixer, whip the cream cheese with the eggs and sugar until smooth. Melt the chocolate and butter together and add to the cream cheese mixture. Add the sour cream, vanilla, salt and walnuts. Mix well and pour into the prepared crust. Bake in a preheated 325° oven for 2 hours. Allow the cake to cool at room temperature and then chill overnight.

Chocolate Cheesecake

Fabulous!

4 (8-ounce) packages Cream Cheese
1½ cups Granulated Sugar
6 Eggs
3 (1-ounce) squares Bitter Chocolate, melted
2 Tbl. fresh Lemon Juice
½ cup Pecans, finely chopped
1½ cups Cool Whip
1½ cups Sour Cream

Slice the cream cheese into cubes and place in a mixer. Beat in the sugar and eggs one at a time. Add the chocolate and lemon juice. Beat until smooth and creamy.

Grease the sides and bottom of 9½" springform pan with Crisco. Sprinkle the pecans along the sides and bottom of the pan. Pour in the batter and bake in a preheated 350° oven for 45 minutes.

Turn off the oven and keep the door closed for 15 additional minutes. When removed from the oven, the cheesecake will not be completely dry. Allow it to cool completely.

Combine the Cool Whip and sour cream and mix well. Spread over the top of the cheesecake.

Grandmother's Fruit Cake

(Yields approximately 14 pounds)

This is a true turn-of-the-century fruit cake – made from scratch! You will want to make it two weeks to a month ahead of serving to allow the flavors to ripen. I have vivid memories of helping my grandmother with this – what a treasure! And it's wonderful when served with boiled custard!

1 pound Light Raisins	1 pound Dark Raisins
1 pound Dates	1 pound Figs
8 ounces Grape Juice	1 pound Flour, sifted
1 pound Butter	1 pound Granulated Sugar
12 Eggs, separated and yolks slightly beaten	8 ounce jar Grape Jelly, warmed in microwave
1 Tbl. Cinnamon	½ tsp. Ground Cloves
1 Tbl. Nutmeg	2 tsp. (½ square) Unsweetened Chocolate, melted
1 pound shelled Almonds (reserve whole pieces for topping)	1 pound shelled Pecans
1 pound Crystallized Cherries	1 pound Crystallized Pineapple
½ pound Citron (crystallized candied citron fruit)	½ pound Orange Paste (only available at a candy store)

Finely cut the fruits and pour the grape juice over the top. Allow the mixture to stand over night, mixing occasionally.

Spread the flour in a shallow baking pan and brown in a preheated 400° oven. Occasionally turn the flour with a spoon to prevent burning.

Cream the butter, sugar and egg yolks. To the warmed jelly add the cinnamon, cloves, nutmeg and chocolate. Add this mixture to the creamed egg yolks. Fold in the egg whites and by hand slowly stir in the nuts, fruit and orange paste. Pour the batter into 1 pound pans lined with aluminum foil. Begin baking in a cold oven uncovered. Bake on 225° for 5½ hours. Do not open the doors during baking. Remove and allow to cool completely.

Dip cheese cloth in wine or grape juice and wrap around each 1 pound cake. Place in an airtight container until ready to serve. You can periodically remove the cheese cloth and again dip it in wine and rewrap the cake. This process helps keep the fruit cake moist through the holiday season.

Dark Chocolate Cheesecake

Basic Crumb Crust:

   1½ cups Graham Cracker Crumbs

   6 Tbl. Butter, melted

   ¼ cup Granulated Sugar

Cheesecake:

   5 (1-ounce) squares Semi-Sweet Chocolate

   24 ounces Cream Cheese

   ¾ cup Granulated Sugar

   3 large Eggs

   1 tsp. Vanilla

   1 cup Sour Cream

Crust: Combine all of the crust ingredients and mix well. Press into the bottom and 2" up the sides of a 10" springform pan. Chill for 5 to 10 minutes.

Cheesecake: Melt the chocolate in the top of a double boiler. Meanwhile, in a large mixing bowl, beat the cream cheese and sugar until smooth and light. Beat in the eggs and vanilla. Stir in the melted chocolate and sour cream. Blend well.

Pour the mixture into the prepared pie crust and bake in a preheated 350° oven for 1 hour 15 minutes. Turn off the heat and allow the cake to cool in the oven. Chill before serving. Top with whipping cream if desired.

Italian Cream Cake

1 stick Butter

½ cup Shortening

2 cups Granulated Sugar

5 Eggs Yolks

2 cups Flour

1 cup Purity Dairy Buttermilk

1 tsp. Baking Soda dissolved in 1½ tsp. Vanilla

5 Egg Whites, beaten until stiff

1 cup Coconut

1 cup Pecans, chopped

Icing:

8 ounces Cream Cheese, softened

½ stick Butter

1 box Powdered Sugar

Toppings:

Coconut Flakes

Whole Pecans

Beat the egg whites until soft peaks form. Set aside. In a separate bowl, cream the butter, shortening and sugar. Add the egg yolks and beat well. In a separate bowl, combine the flour, buttermilk and baking soda/vanilla mixture. Fold in the beaten egg whites, coconut and pecans. Pour the batter into three 9" pans. Bake in a preheated 350° oven for 30 minutes. Allow to cool.

Icing: Combine the cream cheese, butter and powdered sugar. Beat well, adding milk if needed. Ice the cake and then decorate with the coconut flakes and pecans.

Jam Cake

This recipe is very old. Only use a wire whisk to stir — no mixer.

2 cups Margarine, melted

6 Eggs, separated and
    beaten separately

1 tsp. Allspice

2 tsp. Ground Cloves

2 cups Seedless Blackberry Jam

2 cups Granulated Sugar

3 cups Flour

2 tsp. Baking Soda

2 tsp. Cinnamon

1 cup Purity Dairy Buttermilk

Whisk the margarine and sugar until fluffy. Beat in the egg yolks one at a time. In a separate bowl, combine the flour, baking soda, Allspice, cinnamon and cloves. Add the mixture to the butter and egg mixture, alternately with buttermilk. With a spoon, stir in the jam and fold in the beaten egg whites. Bake in a preheated 350° oven for 40 minutes. When the cake is cool, frost with caramel icing.

Caramel Icing:

2 cups packed Light Brown Sugar

3 Tbl. Butter

1 cup Heavy Cream

1 tsp. Vanilla

Combine the brown sugar and heavy cream in a saucepan over medium heat. Cook and stir the mixture until it begins to simmer. Stop stirring, cover and simmer an additional 2 minutes. Uncover and continue cooking until the mixture reaches softball stage — at approximately 238° on a candy thermometer.

Remove from the heat and without stirring, add the butter. Set aside without stirring for 1 hour. Add the vanilla and transfer the mixture to an electric mixer. Beat until the mixture cools and begins to be of spreading consistency. If the icing is too thick, add a bit of heavy cream. If too wet, place the mixing bowl in ice water and continue mixing until desired consistency.

Marble Cheesecake

Graham Cracker Crust:

 1½ cups Graham Cracker Crumbs

 6 Tbl. Butter, melted

 ¼ cup Granulated Sugar

Cheesecake:

 3 (1-ounce) squares Unsweetened Chocolate

 1 tsp. Vegetable Shortening

 2 pounds Cream Cheese

 2 tsp. Vanilla

 1½ cups Granulated Sugar

 6 large Eggs, lightly beaten

 2 cups Light Cream (or 1 cup Heavy Cream and 1 cup Purity Dairy Milk)

Crust: Combine all of the crust ingredients and mix well. Pat into the bottom and sides of a 9½" springform pan. Chill for 10 minutes.

Cheesecake: Melt the chocolate and shortening in the top of a double boiler. Meanwhile, in a large mixing bowl beat the cream cheese and vanilla until light and fluffy. Slowly add the sugar and eggs. Beat just until well blended. Stir in the cream.

In another bowl, separate and pour 3 cups of the cream cheese mixture and add the melted chocolate. Blend well. Pour the remaining cream cheese mixture into the prepared crust. Add the chocolate mixture by dabbing spoonfuls on the top in three areas. Using a knife or spatula, swirl the chocolate mixture through the white mixture in a zigzag motion.

Bake in a preheated 450° oven for 15 minutes. Reduce the temperature to 300° and bake for 1 hour. Allow the cake to cool at room temperature. Chill before serving.

Strawberry Cake

1 box White Cake Mix

4 Eggs

1 small box Strawberry Jell-O

⅔ cups Vegetable Oil

2 cups frozen Strawberries

With a mixer, blend all of the ingredients for 3 minutes. The batter should be fluffy. Pour the batter into a greased 9"x13" Pyrex pan. Bake in a preheated 350° oven for 45 minutes. Allow to cool and top with butter cream frosting (see recipe on page 141).

Vanilla Pound Cake

This wonderful pound cake is so tasty. It is good alone or topped with fruit and whipped cream.

3 sticks Butter, softened

8 ounces Cream Cheese, softened

3 cups Granulated Sugar

6 Eggs

1 Tbl. Vanilla

3 cups Flour

With a mixer, beat the butter until fluffy and light in color. Alternating, slowly add the cream cheese and sugar. Beat in the eggs one at a time and the vanilla. Add the flour ½ cup at a time. Beat the mixture on medium-high for an additional 3 minutes. The batter should be very fluffy. Pour the batter into a greased and floured tube pan and bake in a preheated 300° oven for 1½ hours.

(Compliments of my mother Alyce Scobey)

Homemade Pastry

2¼ cup Flour, sifted

¼ cup Ice Water

¾ cup Shortening

1 tsp. Salt

Combine ⅓ cup of flour with ice water and mix to create a paste. Cut the shortening and the salt into the remaining flour and add to the paste. Roll the dough into a ball, cover with plastic wrap, and refrigerate for 1 hour.

Remove from the refrigerator and divide the dough into two pieces. Roll out the dough on a lightly floured surface to desired size for your pie plate, rolling as thin as possible. Bake in a preheated 425° oven for approximately 15 minutes or until golden.

(Compliments of my sister Suzan Putman,
who happens to be the best pie maker in Nashville!)

Ali's Apple Pie

1 package (2 crusts) refrigerated Pie Crust

6 cups tart, firm Apples, peeled and thinly sliced

1 cup Granulated Sugar

1 tsp. Cinnamon

1 stick Butter, cut into 12 slices

2 Tbl. Butter, melted

Allow the refrigerated pie crusts to soften. Place one pie crust in the bottom of a pie dish. Combine the apples, sugar and cinnamon in a large Zip Lock bag. Shake well until the apples are evenly coated. Pour the apples into the pie pan. Place the butter pieces on top of the apples. Cover the apples with the remaining pie crust. Pinch the sides of the crusts and cut slits in the top. Brush the pie with the melted butter and sprinkle with a bit of sugar.

Place the pie dish on a cookie sheet to catch any overflow and bake in a preheated 375° oven for 1 hour or until the top is golden.

(Compliments of my daughter Ali Burns,
French Pastry School – Chicago)

eet Nothings – Pies

Apricot Pie

This tart pie has just the right amount of sweet! It's absolutely delicious and outstanding if you make your own crust (see page 159).

12 ounce bag Dried Apricots

1 envelope Unflavored Gelatin

1 cup Brown Sugar

½ tsp. Salt

1½ cups Apricot Pulp

1 Tbl. Lemon Juice

3 Eggs, separated

2 Tbl. Granulated Sugar

½ cup Heavy Cream

Pie Shell, pre-baked

Whipped Cream – *for topping*

To make the apricot pulp: In a saucepan, cover the apricots with water and simmer on low for 30 minutes. Drain the apricots, reserving ¼ cup of the apricot water. Mash the softened apricots to a pulp. Measure 1½ cups of the apricot pulp and set aside.

In another saucepan, mix the gelatin, brown sugar and salt. In a separate bowl, combine the apricot pulp, reserved apricot juice, lemon juice and egg yolks. Add this mixture to the gelatin mixture and stir over medium heat just until the mixture begins to boil. Remove from the heat and chill.

Separately beat the egg whites until foamy and add the sugar. Beat until stiff. Separately beat the heavy cream until stiff. Fold together the heavy cream, egg white mixture and the gelatin mixture. Pour the filling into the pie shell and top with whipped cream.

(Compliments of my Aunt Elva Scobey)

Black Bottom Pie

Crust:

18 to 20 Ginger Snap Cookies, crushed

½ stick Butter or Margarine, melted

1 Tbl. Gelatin

¼ cup cold Water

Chocolate Custard Filling:

1½ cup Purity Dairy Milk

½ cup Granulated Sugar

2 Tbl. Cornstarch

4 Egg Yolks, beaten

1½ square Unsweetened Chocolate, melted

1 tsp. Vanilla

Rum Custard Filling:

1½ Tbl. Rum Flavoring

4 Egg Whites

½ cup Granulated Sugar

¼ tsp. Cream of Tartar

Toppings:

½ pint Heavy Whipping Cream

¼ cup Granulated Sugar

3 Tbl. Sweetened Chocolate Shavings

(continued)

Crust: Combine the ginger snaps and butter. Press the mixture into a 9" deep-dish pie pan. Bake in a preheated 350° oven for 10 minutes.

Dissolve the gelatin in the cold water.

Chocolate Custard Filling: Scald (heat until steaming) the milk. Combine the sugar with the cornstarch and add to the scalded milk, stirring well. Slowly pour the hot mixture into the beaten egg yolks. Whisk well and cook over very low heat until the custard coats a spoon and thickens.

Remove from the heat and pour 1 cup of the custard into a separate bowl. Add the melted chocolate and vanilla to the remaining custard. Allow the filling to cool and then pour into the cooled crust and refrigerate.

Rum Custard Filling: Add the dissolved gelatin to the remaining custard while it is still hot. Allow to cool, but not become stiff. Add the rum to the custard.

Make a meringue by beating the egg whites with the remaining ½ cup of sugar and the cream of tarter. Fold the meringue into the cooled custard and gelatin mixture. Smooth the mixture on top of the chocolate custard layer. At this point, the pie can be frozen.

Serve with whipped cream sweetened with the sugar. Garnish with chocolate curls (see page 141). Keep the pie refrigerated.

(Compliments of my friend Carol Boeing)

Heavenly Chocolate Pie

This pie should be made the same day you serve it. Allow 4 hours to chill before serving.

9" Pie Shell, baked

2 Eggs, separated

½ tsp. Vinegar

¼ tsp. plus ⅛ tsp. Cinnamon

¾ cup Granulated Sugar

¼ tsp. Salt

1 cup Semisweet Chocolate Morsels

¼ cup Water

1 cup Heavy Cream

Beat together the egg whites, vinegar, ¼ tsp. cinnamon, ½ cup sugar and salt until stiff. Spread the mixture over the bottom and up the sides of the baked pie shell. Bake in a preheated 325° oven for 18 to 20 minutes or until the meringue is lightly browned.

While the meringue bakes, mix together the chocolate morsels and water. Microwave on high until the chocolate melts. Immediately beat in the egg yolks using a wire whisk. Blend well and cool. Spread half of the chocolate mixture over the cooled meringue. Put the half-filled pie and remaining chocolate mixture in the refrigerator to chill.

When both have chilled, beat the heavy cream until stiff and add the remaining amounts of cinnamon and sugar. Layer half of the whipped cream mixture over the chilled chocolate layer. Return to the refrigerator for 30 minutes.

For the final layer, combine the remaining chocolate mixture and the remaining whipped cream mixture. Dollop the combined mixture in the center of the pie. Chill the pie before serving.

(Compliments of my Aunt Elva Scobey)

Caramel Pie

This is an old-fashioned caramel pie – you even caramelize your sugar!

3 Eggs, separated
1½ cup Granulated Sugar
2 Tbl. Flour
⅛ tsp. Salt
1½ Tbl. Butter
1½ cup Purity Dairy Milk
1 tsp. Vanilla
9" Pie Shell, baked

Meringue:
3 Egg Whites
½ tsp. Cream of Tartar
¾ cup Granulated Sugar

With a hand mixer, beat the egg yolks until light and fluffy.

Separately combine ¾ cup of the sugar and the flour and add to the egg yolk mixture. Add the butter, salt and milk. Mix well and cook in a double boiler until thick.

While this mixture is cooking, caramelize the remaining ¾ cup sugar. Pour the sugar in a black iron skillet over medium heat and brown – careful not to burn. The sugar will liquefy. When the sugar reaches a rapid boil, pour it into the egg mixture in the double boiler and stir constantly until thickened. Remove from the heat and add the vanilla. Pour the mixture into the cooked pie shell and top with the meringue.

Meringue: Beat the egg whites until foamy and then beat in the cream of tartar. Gradually add the sugar and beat until stiff peaks form. Top the pie with the meringue, attaching it first to the edges of the crust and working toward the center of the pie.

Bake in a preheated 325° oven for 20 minutes to brown the meringue to a light golden color.

Chocolate Marvel Pie

9" Pie Shell, baked

6 ounces Chocolate Chips

2 Tbl. Purity Dairy Milk

3 Tbl. Granulated Sugar

4 large Eggs, separated

¼ tsp. Cream of Tartar beaten with 4 Egg Whites

½ tsp. Vanilla

Whipped Cream – *for topping*

In a double boiler, melt the chocolate chips with the milk and sugar. Beat in the egg yolks one at a time and simmer for a minute. Allow the mixture to cool and then add the vanilla.

In a separate bowl, beat the egg whites and cream of tartar until very stiff. Fold the egg white mixture into the cooled chocolate mixture. Mix well and pour the filling into the pie shell and chill for 8 hours. Top with whipped cream.

Cranberry Pie

2 cups Fresh Cranberries

½ cup Granulated Sugar

½ cup Pecans, chopped

1 cup Flour

½ cup Butter, melted

¼ cup Vegetable Oil

2 Eggs

1 cup Granulated Sugar

1 cup Whipping Cream – *for topping*

Sprinkle the cranberries over the bottom of a greased deep-dish baking pan. Sprinkle the sugar and pecans on top of cranberries.

Premix the flour, butter and shortening. In a separate bowl, beat the eggs well and gradually add the sugar. Add this mixture to the flour mixture, mix well, and pour over the cranberries.

Bake in a preheated 325° oven for 50 minutes. Top with fresh whipped cream.

Lemon Meringue Pie

So good!

9" Pie Shell, baked

Filling:

1 cup Granulated Sugar

⅓ cup Cornstarch

¼ tsp. Salt

1½ cups Hot Water

4 Egg Yolks, slightly beaten

2 Tbl. Butter

6 ounce can Frozen Lemonade

Meringue:

4 Egg Whites, room temperature

¼ tsp. Cream of Tartar

½ cup Granulated Sugar

In a saucepan, combine the sugar, cornstarch and salt. Slowly stir in the hot water. Add the remaining filling ingredients and cook over low heat until the mixture comes to a full boil. Lower the heat and cook a minute longer. Cool until lukewarm. Spread the filling into the pie shell.

Meringue: Beat the egg whites and cream of tarter until soft peaks form. Add the sugar a tablespoon at a time, beating until stiff peaks form.

Spread the meringue on top of the lemon filling and bake in a preheated 325° oven for 20 to 25 minutes, or until lightly brown.

(Compliments of my sister Suzan Putman)

Mincemeat Pie

Be brave and try this – you'll be pleasantly surprised!

9" Pie Shell, unbaked

1 large Tart Apple, peeled and diced

half a 1 pound can Red Sour Cherries, pitted and drained

¼ cup Brandy or Sherry

1 cup Granulated Sugar

½ tsp. Cinnamon

1 pound jar Mincemeat (Crosse & Blackwell)

2 Tbl. Butter

⅓ cup Flour

Marinate the apples and cherries in brandy or sherry for 4 hours. In a separate bowl, combine ½ cup of sugar and the cinnamon. Mix well and set aside.

Drain the apples and cherries and combine with the sugar and cinnamon mixture. Stir in the mincemeat. Mix well and pour the filling into the pie shell. In a separate bowl, cut the butter into the flour and add the remaining sugar. Sprinkle the crumbly topping over the mincemeat.

Bake in a preheated 450° oven for 15 minutes. Reduce the heat to 350° and bake for an additional 30 minutes. Eat the same day.

Boston Cream Pie

1 box yellow Cake Mix (Prepared, but use only 1 cake round. Allow to cool and cut the 1 layer into 2 thin layers. Freeze the remaining layer for later use.)

1 cup Heavy Cream, cold

½ cup Half-and-Half

3 ounce package Instant Vanilla Pudding Mix, unprepared

½ cup Chocolate Icing, softened in microwave (see page 119)

On low speed, beat the heavy cream and Half-and-Half with the instant pudding mix until it is very thick. Make sure the cake layer is very cold and spread the cream mixture over one of the thin cake layers. Place the remaining thin cake layer on top of the cream.

Prepare the icing and pour over the top cake layer.

Mother's Chess Pie

9" Pie Shell, unbaked

4 Egg Yolks, beaten until light

½ cup Butter

1½ cup Granulated Sugar

2 Tbl. Flour

1 cup Purity Dairy Milk

1 tsp. Vanilla

dash of Salt

Combine all of the ingredients and heat in a sauce pan until warm, beating constantly with a hand mixer. Pour the filling into the pie shell and bake in a preheated 350° oven for 45 minutes.

(Compliments of my mother Alyce Scobey)

Nana's Crustless Fudge Pie

2 sticks Margarine

2 cups Granulated Sugar

½ cup Cocoa

½ cup Flour

pinch of Salt

2 tsp. Pure Vanilla

4 Eggs, beaten

Almonds, toasted *(optional)*

Melt the margarine in a 9"x13" Pyrex dish in a preheated 350° oven.

In a separate bowl, combine the dry ingredients and mix in the melted margarine. Add the vanilla and eggs. Mix well. Pour the mixture back into the Pyrex dish and bake in the preheated 350° oven for 25 minutes.

Serve the warm pie with ice cream, hot fudge sauce (see to page 134), and toasted almonds if desired.

(Compliments of employee Martha Page)

Notes:

Roses at Beynac, collection of Lassie McDonald Crowder.
Roses in the medieval town of Beynac, France, in Perigord.

7-Layer Dip

A delicious and popular appetizer – perfect for any occasion.

3 (9-ounce) cans Bean Dip

1 package (1.25 ounce) Taco Seasoning

16 ounces Sour Cream

2 Avocados, peeled and thinly sliced

2 cups total Cheddar and Monterey Jack Cheeses combined, finely shredded

2 (2.5-ounce) cans Chopped Black Olives

4 ounce can chopped Jalapeño Peppers

2 to 3 Tomatoes, diced

Spread the bean dip in the bottom of an ungreased casserole dish. Mix the taco seasoning with the sour cream and spread it over the bean dip. Layer the avocado slices next and sprinkle with lemon juice to prevent avocados from turning bown. Next layer the remaining ingredients – ending with the tomatoes. Refrigerate for 2 hours. Serve with tortilla chips.

(Compliments of my daughter Kristi Stone Elzinga)

Homemade Salsa

7 pounds Ripe Tomatoes – peeled, drained, smashed

1 pound Onions, chopped

½ cup Apple Cider Vinegar

1 tsp. Pepper

6 Jalapeño Peppers, chopped

1 Tbl. Salt

Mix all of the ingredients and heat in a saucepan until thick. Allow to cool and store in the refrigerator. Serve with tortilla chips.

Festive Salsa

Prepare this tasty salsa several hours before serving to allow the flavors to meld.

2 (10-ounce) cans Rotel Tomatoes with Green Chilies

2 (15-ounce) cans Diced Tomatoes

15 ounce can Black Beans, rinsed and drained

14½ ounce can Yellow Corn, drained

½ bunch Green Onions, finely chopped

1 bunch Fresh Cilantro, finely chopped

3 Garlic Cloves, minced

½ tsp. Ground Cumin

1 Tbl. Lime Juice

Salt to taste

Combine all of the ingredients and refrigerate. Serve with tortilla chips.

(Compliments of my daughter Kristi Stone Elzinga)

Puffy Muffin Ginger Tea

3 heaping Tbl. Instant Tea (plain, no sugar, no lemon)

1½ cups Granulated Sugar

6 cups warm Water

2 cups diluted Orange Juice

6 ounce can frozen Limeade, undiluted

2 liters Ginger Ale (or enough to make 1 gallon)

Combine the instant tea, sugar and water. Stir well to ensure the sugar is dissolved. Add the orange juice and Limeade. Refrigerate until ready to serve.

Just before serving, add enough Ginger Ale to make 1 gallon of liquid. If you prefer sweeter tea, omit 1 to 2 cups of the Ginger Ale.

Hot Instant Spiced Tea Mix

21 ounces Tang

15 ounces Dry Lemonade

6 ounces dry Instant Iced Tea

1½ cup Granulated Sugar

1½ tsp. Cinnamon

¾ tsp. Ground Cloves

¾ tsp. Nutmeg

¾ tsp. Allspice

Combine all of the ingredients and mix well. Store in an airtight container until ready for use.

To each cup of boiling water, add 2 spoonfuls of the dry tea mix. Depending on desired strength, add less or more tea mix.

Pineapple Spread

12 ounces Cream Cheese

1 Tbl. Onion, minced

8 ounce can Crushed Pineapple, drained

Lawreys Seasoning Salt to taste

In a mixer, beat the cream cheese until fluffy. Add the remaining ingredients and mix with a spoon. Chill and serve with Sociable crackers.

Puffy Muffin Artichoke Dip

Make the day before serving and serve hot with tortilla chips.

1¼ cups Artichokes, drained and coarsely chopped

8 ounces frozen Chopped Spinach, thawed and squeezed dry

1 cup Mayonnaise

½ cup Onion, chopped

1¼ cups Parmesan Cheese

¾ tsp. Garlic Powder

¾ tsp. Pepper

¾ tsp. Salt

1 cup Half-and-Half

1 cup Heavy Cream

Swiss Cheese, shredded – *topping*

Combine all of the main ingredients and mix well with a spoon. Let the dip sit in the refrigerator overnight.

The next day, place the dip in a greased casserole dish and sprinkle the top with cheese. Bake in a preheated 350° oven for 30 minutes or until bubbly. If you choose to heat the dip in the microwave, cover with plastic wrap.

Stuffed Mushrooms

12 Mushrooms, 2" diameter or larger

1 medium Onion, chopped

2 ounces Pepperoni, chopped

1 small Garlic Clove, minced

¼ cup Green Pepper, minced

2 Tbl. Butter

½ cup (12) Ritz Crackers, crushed

3 Tbl. Parmesan Cheese

1 Tbl. Parsley, chopped

½ tsp. Salt

¼ tsp. Oregano

⅓ cup Chicken Broth

Wash the mushrooms and remove the stems. Finely chop the stems only. In a blender chop the onions, pepperoni, garlic, green pepper and chopped mushroom stems.

Melt the butter and sauté the mixture until tender. Add the crackers, parmesan cheese, parsley, salt, oregano and chicken broth. Stir well. Spoon the mixture into the washed and dried mushroom caps and place in a shallow pan with ¼" water. Bake uncovered in a preheated 325° oven for 25 minutes.

Texas Caviar

14.5 ounce can Shoe Peg Corn

1 Green Pepper, chopped

14.5 ounce can Black Beans, rinsed and drained

14.5 ounce can Pinto Beans, rinsed and drained

4 ounce can Green Chilies, chopped

1 Garlic Clove, chopped

1 Sweet Onion, chopped

2 Roma Tomatoes, chopped

8 ounce bottle Fat Free Italian Dressing

Combine all of the ingredients except for the dressing. Mix well and add the dressing. Cover and chill for 2 hours. Serve with tortilla chips.

(Compliments of my daughter Ali Burns,
French Pastry School – Chicago)

Cho[...]

Fantastic when ser[...]

8 ounces Crea[...]

½ cup Butter,

½ tsp. Vanilla

¾ cup Powder[...]

2 Tbl. Brown S[...]

¾ cup Semi-S[...]

¾ cup pecans,

[handwritten notes overlaid:]
8 oz. cream cheese
½ c butter
vanilla
brown sugar
semi-sweet mini choc. chips
pecans, finely chopped
graham crackers

In a mixer, beat [...] fluffy. Gradually add the sugars. Beat until well combined. Stir in chocolate chips. Cover and refrigerate for 2 hours. Shape the mixture into a ball. Refrigerate for 1 hour. Roll in the pecans. Serve with graham crackers.

(Compliments of Shani McMurtry)

Cheese & Beef Dip

1 pound lean Ground Beef

1 packet Taco Seasoning

¾ cup Water

4 (8-ounce) blocks Cream Cheese, softened to room temperature

2 to 3 cups Cheddar Cheese, shredded

Brown the ground beef and drain any fat. Stir in the taco seasoning and water. Bring the mixture to a boil, then reduce the heat and simmer for 5 minutes, stirring occasionally.

Spread the cream cheese in the bottom of an ungreased 8½"x11" casserole dish. Pour the ground beef mixture over the cream cheese. Sprinkle the cheese over the beef and bake in a preheated 300° oven for 30 minutes or until bubbly. Serve warm with tortilla chips.

(Compliments of Shani McMurtry)

Herbed Sausage Rolls

2 (8-ounce) cans refrigerated Crescent Rolls

2 Tbl. Margarine, melted

¼ cup Parmesan Cheese, grated

1 tsp. Dried Oregano

32 "Little Smokies" Sausage Links

Separate both cans of crescent rolls into 4 rectangles each. Press to seal the perforations. Cut each of the 8 rectangles into 4 pieces. Brush the dough with butter. Combine the cheese and oregano and sprinkle the mixture over the butter.

Place a sausage link on each piece of dough and roll it up. Place the sausage rolls on an ungreased cookie sheet and bake in a preheated 375° oven for 15 minutes.

(Compliments of Sandy Jones)

Apple-Shaped Cheese Ball

Great appetizer for fall!

8 ounces Cream Cheese, softened

8 ounces White Cheddar Cheese, grated

1 tsp Garlic Powder

⅛ tsp. Ground Cayenne Pepper

Paprika

1 Cinnamon Stick, broken in half

2 Bay Leaves

With a mixer, combine the first 4 ingredients until just blended. Chill for 30 minutes. Form into a ball and chill another 30 minutes. Roll the cheese ball in the paprika until covered.

Flatten the top of the ball by pressing 2 to 4 thumbprints in the center to shape similar to an apple. Place half of a cinnamon stick through the top to resemble a stem. Garnish with bay leaves to resemble apple leaves. Serve with crackers of your choice.

(Compliments of Sandy Jones)

Cheese Krispies

(Yields approximately 75 wafers)

This recipe should be made by hand – no mixer.

- **1 tsp. Cayenne Pepper**
- **1 tsp. Salt**
- **3 cups Flour, sifted**
- **1½ cups Butter, softened to room temperature**
- **3 cups Sharp Cheddar Cheese, finely grated**
- **1½ cup Rice Krispies**

Add the cayenne pepper and salt to the sifted flour. Cut the butter into the flour mix. Work the mixture between your fingers to produce a cornmeal-like consistency. Add the cheese and Rice Krispies. Continue to combine with your fingers. The more you mix, the more "butter-like" the dough will become and will better hold the Krispies together.

Roll the dough into 1" balls, working in your hands to press the balls together. Place on a cookie sheet lined with parchment paper. Press the balls flat with a fork or the bottom of a flour covered glass. Bake in a preheated 350° oven for 15 minutes or until golden.

After completely cooled, store in an airtight container.

The Puffy Muffin Crew

Left to Right Back Row: General Manager Jason Burns; Shana Rogers; Rachel Hillin, Mary Lauren Whitehead, Cammie Allen, Kristen Richey, Tina Allen, Sherry Farr, Jason Valentine, Clint Akins, Ron Fisher, Ali Burns, Elizabeth Starpoli, Debbie Huggard, Sam Tucker; Fernando Rodriguez, Dell Sartin, Kaela Fourkiller, Marielle Jung, Werner Bacher, Lynda Stone - Center Row, Left to Right, Seated: Pam Butler; Marcy Batterton, Beverly Puckett, Jennifer Anneken, Anne Starpoli, Doug Dabbs, Martha Page

Not Pictured: Christine Anneken, Andrew Butler, Linda Gaw, Christy Kerinuk, Deby Leahy, Heriberto Lopez, Jennifer Martin, Rusti Meng, Alexandra Mattea, Chad Milliken, Genevieve Mogan, Ray Ng, Landon Sartin, Joe Spann, Ezequiel Tepox, Nicole Todd, Rebecca Wilson

Managers
Left to Right, Standing: Kitchen Manager, Jason Valentine; Register Supervisor, Kaela
Fourkiller; Pastry Manager, Werner Bacher; Front-End Manager, Marcy Batterton; Left
Right, Seated: Cake Decorating Manager, Ali Burns; Server Supervisor, Pam Butler;
General Manager, Jason Burns; Delivery Manager, Jennifer Anneken

The Bakery
Sam Tucker, Chef Werner Bacher, Alexandra Mattea

Line Staff
Front to Back: Ezequiel Tepox, Debbie Huggard, Fernando Rodriguez, Jason Valentine

Cake Decorators
Elizabeth Starpoli and Ali Burns

Top row, left to right: John Elzinga, Jack Stone and Jason Burns.

Bottom row, left to right: Jackson Elzinga, Kristi Elzinga, Mason Elzinga, Lynda Stone,
Ali Burns, Hannah Burns and Matthew Burns.

Index

SIDES THAT SIZZLE

SWEET NOTHINGS:

Cookies & Candy:

Notes:

Notes: